Liz
you ma

Power Up, Super Women

MOTIVATION
CHAMPS
PUBLISHING

Copyright 2019 Motivation Champs Publishing
ISBN-10: 1-7323621-6-5
ISBN-13: 978-1-7323621-6-1

Power Up, Super Women

Manufactured in the United States of America

For information about special discounts for bulk orders or speaking engagements, please contact
motivationchamps@gmail.com

Pictured on cover of book, from left to right:

Top row - *Dr. Renée Galloway, Dr. Kelly Donohoe, Charlotte Bowman Murphy, Jenny Lynn Hood*

2nd row from top - *Lynnis Woods-Mullins, Sonali Dutta, Amy C. Waninger, Olivia Solomon*

3rd row from top - *Jeanny Chai, Jonamay Lambert, Tracey S. Yang, Jodie Edmiston, Sarika Bhakta, CDE*

Bottom row - *Aline Yska, Cherie Faus-Smith, Sunayana Dumala, Nicole Jansen*

TABLE OF CONTENTS

Foreword

I'm delighted and honored to write the foreword for this anthology book. Some amazingly talented and passionate women from different walks of life have shared their life experiences to inspire and motivate women around the world. I personally thank Dominick for connecting these authors and driving this project on women empowerment through his organization, Motivation Champs, and providing a medium to share their success stories.

As a woman, I believe this book is very much needed for all of us to collectively learn and pass on those necessary life lessons to other women. Not only to improve our lives but also to collaboratively lift the society to make a difference in this world. Even though women have time and again proved that we are able and capable of breaking the glass walls, the sad reality is that even in 21st century, we are still having to face discrimination, sexual harassment, and many other social barriers, which leaves us powerless and oppressed. In addition, women being perceived as weak and vulnerable often leads to exploitation at both personal and professional levels.

The essence of this book is to help address some of these challenges by inspiring and empowering women. This anthology book is a conglomeration of powerful diverse stories, and each chapter focuses on a unique subject. It felt both heartwarming and touching to read these personal stories, as I could relate my own life to theirs at many circumstances—being bullied, being molested, being timid, being uncomfortable in larger groups, and being a victim. I had to work very hard to overcome these barriers at different phases of my life. I am certainly positive that you would also feel the same when reading this book and relate to these authors—how they struggled to overcome their life obstacles just like you.

My immigrant journey was not as easy as I anticipated, coming from India to Midwest America. Having to adjust to a new culture being far away from family made it even tougher. I was born and raised in India in a middle-class family. Being the youngest of three daughters, I was also the most pampered and protected one in the family. I grew up envisioning the U.S. as the land of dreams. I took the brave step of immigrating to the U.S. in my early 20s to pursue my master's degree to become a strong, independent woman. And as many of you may have experienced, I even had many diversions during this phase of my journey, but I continued to work through my goals with the same level of determination and dedication until my dreams came into fruition.

But I knew I could not have done it all alone, and I am fortunate to have my husband who filled in the shoes of my family in their absence here in the U.S. I felt blessed to have him in my life, both as a friend and a mentor. He worked on my weaknesses and guided me to surpass them by focusing on my strengths. He never shied away from providing critical feedback and always trusted in my capabilities. After completing my master's, I did not get a job immediately, and being an immigrant who would need work visa sponsorship made it further difficult to obtain a job. I was unemployed for four years because of the visa regulations. It felt miserable to not be able to give back to the community and make use of my education. But my husband always instilled positive thoughts in me to stay focused and optimistic, and if not for him, I would have been broken. When I finally got my current job as a database developer for a Kansas-based pharmaceutical marketing agency, I felt proud of myself, seeing my hard work paid through.

I personally was very happy with my normal routine of going to my day job, coming back home and to my husband, preparing meals, and getting ready for another exciting day the next morning. Both I and my husband were also looking forward to extending our family. But an unexpected tragedy hit me when my husband was murdered in a horrific hate crime. This incident shattered my life, as I had lost the most precious thing in my life—my rock, my support, my husband. But instead of being angry and resentful, I chose to embrace positivity. Soon, I found that being surrounded by loving family, friends, and community made me stronger and gave me the courage to continue with my life. It is natural for us to be afraid of change, but when we are forced to change, we strive to put our best foot forward and try to succeed. With new-found courage and strength, I found a voice for myself and started advocating to raise awareness on immigrants and stop more hate crimes. This message was my inspiration for starting the Facebook initiative Forever Welcome. This is how I wanted to honor my husband and continue his legacy—by generating empathy, love, and kindness.

Lastly, I would say that success does not come easy, but it is important to have the perseverance to work through each failure and ultimately succeed. It is only when you fail that you will know how to succeed and cherish it. It is also equally important that we are happy and content in whatever we do, as life is too short to let it go. And if we are unable to find that happiness, we will also fail to contribute toward having a happy or stronger community. As I mentioned in the beginning of this foreword, I am certain that after reading this book, you will agree with me that each of these stories reflects your own dreams and the struggles and hardships you had to go through to fulfill them. And if you are one of those who are timid and afraid of taking risks, you might be able to find that courage and motivation to chase those suppressed dreams or explore your forgotten hobbies. I hope everyone who reads the book finds a new level of desire and strength to empower themselves and also those around them.

Sunayana Dumala

CHAPTER 1

The Power of Your Personal Vision

Dr. Renée Galloway

One of the greatest lessons that I can share to help empower women of any age is the importance of having a personal vision. Not a family vision or one that your parents or friends have designed for you but your own vision.

Every book, invention, business, begins with an idea, which is a vision. In the famous words of Henry David Thoreau, "Go in the direction of your dreams! Live the life you've imagined." Can you envision or imagine your ideal life? I wish that I could say that I chose my vision, but my vision actually chose me. Through life's twists and turns, over time, I did embrace it.

I'll give you the Readers Digest® version of my personal journey along the road to birthing one aspect of my big picture vision, and that's Dr. Renée Galloway the Author. The release of my book happened in spite of detours and roadblocks along the journey of life, and yours can also lead to a successful 'personal' outcome.

You may notice that I've mentioned the word 'personal vision' several times. We often hear that it's not about you or me and that it's selfish to think about yourself. Nothing can be further from the truth. Until we are the best person that we can be personally, I don't believe that we are fully able to share the best 'us' with others.

When our personal vision aligns with our core values, likes, hobbies, and passions, that's when the sky is the limit, and nothing is impossible. Although that's not quite enough to make it happen. We must get out of our own way and silence the doubt in our head by first eliminating comparisons from the equation. Comparisons are the arch enemy of visions, dreams, and productivity. When we compare ourselves to others, we don't have the full picture of all the blood, sweat, and tears those individuals have shed to even get to that point. We are judging them by the chapter in their life that we walked in on. Let the journey begin ...

I graduated early from high school at 16 and now realize that I wasn't fully equipped maturity-wise for college but attended anyway. I completed 54 of the 60 credits needed for the associate degree that I was pursuing but still quit. After 10 years of working in a stable job with above average pay for my duties, I realized that I wanted, rather I needed, more. This would lead me to go back to the same school that I had started ten years earlier to complete my bachelor's degree. I didn't take into consideration that I was now the mom of a five-year-old and newly divorced woman and how this would be much different than when I started right out of high school to pursue my degree. Some may see this as a foolish move, but I was still young and confident enough to believe I could do it.

After taking classes spring, summer, winter, and fall, I completed my bachelor's degree in seven years by taking one and sometimes two classes at a time while working full-time and raising my son. The child-like excitement of walking across the stage at graduation was only surpassed by the feeling of being a new mom.

My thirst for knowledge was piqued during this educational pursuit, although I didn't pursue my MBA until three years later. I completed the MBA while again working full time—this time, in an accelerated degree program which I completed in two years. I took advantage of my workplace tuition assistance program, along with the University's promissory note agreement that allowed me to pay for my classes after the semester ended and with a grade of B or better. This sweet arrangement allowed me to graduate with zero debt because I put the tuition on my credit card in order to receive my grades and promptly paid it off when I received the reimbursement from my employer.

The joy of this grand accomplishment was short-lived because, within eight weeks, I received a letter that my job was being eliminated. In fact, the entire department was being eliminated, so it wasn't personal. I was forced to take a step back and evaluate my future. The operative word here was that I was forced to make the change, and it didn't feel good. Within six months and one week, before my unemployment compensation ended, I started a new job. This time, I had a new mindset about working. There was a strong will and level of determination that I hadn't felt in the past. I had super 'shero' power and determination that if I could help it, my future would never again be in the hands of an employer. This determination was two-fold; I would first have a personal vision/strategy for my life that would be ever evolving. Secondly, I would keep my finger on the pulse of my own career. I'm sure there were warning signs that my long-time employment was about to conclude, but I ignored them until probably when all of the management employees were given a copy of the book by the now late author Dr. Spencer Johnson, Who Moved My Cheese?—a parable on change. You would have thought we would pick up on the not-so-subtle hint. If you've not read the book and want to take a fun look at change, pick up a copy; it can be read in a couple of hours. Thirdly, no more complacency or procrastination; both are the arch enemy of productivity.

After landing a new job, I again leveraged the tuition assistance program of my new employer to pursue a doctoral degree in Administrative & Policy Studies—Higher Education Administration—which I completed in 6½ years, again nonstop until completion. Again, the driving factor was to position myself to be in a place where my skills and education, coupled with determination and discipline, would at a minimum provide options that without them would have slim possibilities.

It was after I completed my doctoral degree that I was continually being asked how I did it. I would always respond by saying:

"Do what?" I hadn't stopped to think about my achievements as something extraordinary or unique but can only remember forging ahead to complete my goals with a strong support system of family and friends by my side. This brings to mind a very important point. Critical to personal and professional success is surrounding yourself with people that will celebrate with and believe in you, no matter what it looks like right now. Distance yourself from negativity. Often times, it's the negative perceptions that stay with us much longer than the positive ones. It's important that our support system consists of both champions and cheerleaders. What's the difference? I see a champion as someone who will rally around you but give you sound advice or mentoring. A cheerleader will be there with you every step of the way on your personal/professional journey to uplift you when you're feeling down and celebrate with pom-poms in hand and the victory chant.

But now, when asked, I realize that alongside the support system was determination and discipline. This led me to write my book, *Done! A Guide to… Prioritize, Plan & Accomplish Your Goals*. With the services of a book coach, I was able to take a computer full of notes, presentations, and random thoughts and turn them into a short but concise guide to goal setting and, more importantly, saying "Done!"

I now realize that pursuing my educational and training goals while working full-time was accomplished in three, sometimes not-so-easy, steps: Prioritize, Plan, and Perform. These three high-level categories also include subcategories. For example:

Prioritize:
- Set big picture priorities
- Write your personal vision statement
- Time budgeting, including identifying time stealers

Plan:
- Planning 101
- Win the war on procrastination
- Use of S.M.A.R.T. goals

Perform:

- Take action
- Exercise discipline
- FOCUS = Follow One Course Until Successful

Using the Prioritize-Plan-Perform strategy, while not automatic, can lead to the fulfillment of desired goals and plans.

If you take nothing else away from my story, remember that every, not just some or even most, successful idea, invention, book, business venture—well, you get the picture—started in seed form as a vision. Successful ventures don't just happen automatically or without a physical and financial investment. As much as we recognize that, if asked, most will say that they already know this—these are the same factors that oftentimes keep people from actively pursuing their goals.

I share my story not to impress but to inspire others to do the work that it takes to live their best lives. My mom instilled in me and my siblings growing up that you can achieve anything that you desire if you're willing to 'work.' Throughout life, over and over, I definitely found this to be true when pursuing my goals.

While your life will not look like my life, and my life won't look like the next person's life, one thing is sure, there's a 'better' person inside of each of us. There's a better career, better physical condition, better financial position, better relationship, better family/friends, and more. What's your better? When you identify your 'better,' then determine today what you are willing to do to take the first step toward making it happen. Tools to support betterment goals may include: "accept the need for risk," invest in your personal growth, hire a professional coach, enlist the help of an accountability partner, and seek fresh perspectives, to name a few. Remember, there's no completion without a beginning! Think of the big picture but always keep in mind that there are steps to fulfilling a big picture priority.

In closing, nothing happens overnight for anyone, although it may sometimes look like it to those on the outside looking in. Recognize your personal greatness. Yes, I'm talking to you. With our thoughts, feelings, and actions all working in concert, we're now on the right track to realizing our goals and dreams. Next, prioritize, determine what's important to you, plan, set a goal as well as a strategy, and then perform, take that all-important action step to accomplish your goals. Yes, you, too, can say: "Done!"

ABOUT RENÉE GALLOWAY

What started out as informal coaching and consulting over 20 years ago soon grew into something bigger than she anticipated. Pursuing and completing her higher education goals while working full-time, Galloway managed to remain faithful to her volunteer efforts and work in the ministry.

While many people choose to prioritize their schedules according to what's important, Dr. Renée Galloway knows firsthand that it's even more vital that one is intentional about scheduling priorities. As a serial entrepreneur, author and coach, she not only works with entrepreneurs of all backgrounds to help them define their purpose and passion—she's committed to staying in the birthing room with them until the point of dream fulfillment and delivery. Her proven success strategies of goal setting, time management and action plans have catapulted small and large business owners alike to new levels of success, no matter where they are in their entrepreneurial endeavors.

Through her book, *Done! Prioritize, Plan and Perform to Accomplish Your Goals,* she gives readers a blueprint for not only strategy and direction for business success, but also tangible action steps to aid them in accomplishing goals in real-time. Recognized as a 2016 New Pittsburgh Courier Woman of Excellence, her mission and purpose is crystal clear: to empower others to live their very best life, and achieve personal and professional success—one strategic initiative at a time.

Website: www.sweetinspirationsllc.com

CHAPTER 2

We All Have a Story

Jodie Edmiston

We all have a story, and you never know the untold part of someone else's. Too many judge a book by its cover, and sometimes that's not accurate or fair. I have been told that I'm so lucky to have it all together and that I'm so strong and positive. I guess I am lucky at this point in my life, but it has not always been that way. It's actually been far from it. I had to grow up at a very young age and was always protecting others. I lived in fear and defense mode a lot of the time. Many of my childhood memories are of fear, sadness, mental and physical pain. I felt I could never give or be good enough. In her second marriage, I would see my mom be physically and mentally abused but could not do anything to help. This went on till I was around eight or nine years old. My mother finally, at her breaking point, stood up for us both and never looked backed. It took a few years, but she admitted that this man was the father of my younger brother, but not to me. I learned that I had a father that I had never met from her first marriage that I also knew nothing about. This was a relief, as I now knew that I did nothing wrong but simply was treated this way because I was not his biological daughter. Although I wanted everyone to like me, it was still very hard for me to be able to trust people. I became a people pleaser and put my own feelings on the back burner.

When I got into my mid-teens, I ended up with a boyfriend that was controlling, and I thought he was perfect. This is what I grew up being comfortable with, and it was all that I knew. When I finally dated some guys that were truly good guys, I was always waiting for the shoe to drop. I couldn't understand how someone could be so nice to me. I was uncomfortable in the relationship. I am telling this part of my story because this is what molded me into the person that I was for most of my life. These feelings and fears were embedded in my mind; they were a part of me—or so I thought. When I share this with people who want help with their own life story, they look at me with surprise. I guess they judged this book by its cover.

Fast forward to 2015, I was introduced to some people that were complete opposites of the way I thought. At this point in life, I was a negative nelly and always saw myself as the victim in any bad situation. I wasn't 'living' my life. I was always thinking of what I didn't want and comparing myself to others, even jealous at times. I used anger as a defense mechanism and refused to allow people into my emotions. I was surviving, not thriving; there is a difference. I attracted the same kind of people in my life. Those people would just add to all my negative actions and fuel my circulating emotions. Are you starting to notice a pattern here?

Jeffery Combs, the president and CEO of Golden Mastermind Seminars Inc., had an event in 2017 where he empowered others and coached them to live a better life by design. It wasn't until I attended this event that I finally realized what was going on. As he spoke, I felt he was making references directly to me about my own life. I decided right then and there that I was done living that way. As soon as I got home, I bought a book on CD, *The SECRET*, by Rhonda Byrne. I listened to that every time I was in the car. After I finished it the first time, I put what I learned into action. She showed me how to use the "law of attraction" to my advantage, like so many famous and amazing people already have, instead of against myself. I started stating what I want at least twice a day; once before I got out of bed, and once before I fell asleep. I would be very specific in what I wanted to appear—money, people, a trip, good health, and more good things. I learned that I had to let go of those who did not empower me, those that lived in the state of overwhelm, negativity, fear, and anger. I had to let go of those who felt they needed all that in their lives.

As the days passed, I started attracting what I was envisioning and invited it into my life. I was starting and finishing each day like I was living in abundance already. I was attracting the money that I needed, the employees I needed, and the reactions I needed. My days were being filled with comfort and positivity instead of overwhelm and negativity. I now handle the negative in a different way. I do not give it power or live by dwelling on it. I know that by giving it the energy of me thinking about it, it just invites more of what I don't want. While I cannot control all situations, I can control all my reactions. If something bad happens, I no longer feel like curling up into a ball and crying. I think about how I can fix it and how I will not let that happen again. I know I deserve better, and I am committed to having it. I have learned to live each day in a relaxed state. I wake up grateful and go to bed thankful.

Try this: Think of the situations where something bad happened to you. How did you handle it? Did you go into the victim mode, the "Oh why me" or the "I can't go on like this"? What happened? Did it seem that more negative came to you? Perhaps more stress and depression also. Like attracts like, so what you put out for the world is exactly what you are going to get back. I know for me it would cause a ripple effect, and if it happened in the morning, look out, my whole day would be ruined! Then there are those people that aren't kind, the ones who only ACT happy for you. They are the ones who are all too glad to talk about you behind your back. How about those who will make you angry and resentful? I had to stop and think, *What happens when I get upset over these people? Does my anger, sadness, or offense change anything? No!* Reacting in that way does not do anything but gives them more power over me. I gave them what they wanted by reacting this way. I decided to take all those negative feelings and let go of them. By letting go of it all, I regained my power. I regained control of my reaction and got rid of the power they had over me.

At this point, you either get it, or you're thinking, Blah, blah, blah, whatever! I can relate. I was actually one of those eye-rollers. I thought I knew it all. I just let life happen and thought I had to accept it. It wasn't until I gave in to the fact that things were not working the way they were, and I deserved more. I just decided to change what I was doing and take a chance on a new mindset. I wasn't happy where I was in life mentally, financially, or emotionally, so what was there to lose? It couldn't hurt to believe and put into action what I had learned through *The SECRET* and through the motivation and mindset tools and trainings. I learned really quick that you achieve what you believe. What you have to understand first is that the mind is a powerful tool. It's a tool that when used properly can do amazing things. On the opposite end, though, if the mind is not used in the right way, it can bring you down. I think of the mind as a tool that could make or break you. The way your mind works for you is completely up to you. Nobody can make the changes you need in order to create your reality except you. You can't let others create your relations; you need to live with ease, without chaos and distress. Never give someone else the power to control you. Know that you are worth it, that you are enough, and never let somebody else define you!

I felt I needed to share my story because I know there are more people like the old me out there who deserve to learn and put into action what I have. If I have anything to suggest to you, it'd be to change your mindset to work to your advantage. If you are stuck in a rut, why not make a change? You can't have change unless you are willing to make it. If you take anything away from this chapter, I hope that it is: You are in control of your own reality; you just have to practice taking control. You must believe it to achieve it; live like it's yours already. You become what you believe. Your mind can't tell the difference between reality and what you are just thinking; it's called "fake it until you make it." This is the big one; I read it in a book one time, and it makes sense: "life isn't happening to you; it's reacting to you."

ABOUT JODIE EDMISTON

Jodie Edmiston is passionate about life, family, fitness, and empowering others to be the best version of themselves. Jodie is married to her husband, Brian, and mother of three wonderful children, Dakota, Hunter, and Mackenzie. She enjoys working out, spending time with her family, and listening to books on CD about mindset, self-help, and empowerment.

Jodie is a registered nurse, certified fitness trainer, transformation coach, and vision board trainer. Also certified in fitness nutrition, Jodie is the owner-operator of New Horizons Preschool/Daycare. Her most notable achievements are her two sons and daughter. She has led many clubs and business groups, including empowering networkers.

Jodie is a member of the Chamber and holds a position on the school board. She strives to live life to the fullest and share with others how to do the same. She looks forward to her upcoming Vision Board trainings, her next book, and transforming lives.

Jodie Edmiston lives in Derry, Pennsylvania. To follow her and see what else she is up to, go to:

Website: Fitbyjodie.com

Email: fitbyjodie@gmail.com

Facebook: www.facebook.com/jodie.edmiston.5

CHAPTER 3

Radical Selfishness: A Manifesto

Dr. Kelly Rabenstein Donohoe

People ask me deep questions in my work. Meaningful questions. Meaning-of-life questions. Obviously, I do not have the answers. And yet my patients sometimes need things from me I cannot provide. In the middle ground, I move past anxiety into action. Not empty action full of platitudes but meaningful connections that (I hope) lead others to their next steps. And in the space between "I surely do not know" and "What should we do here?" there can be enough anxiousness to fill my whole insides.

When faced with a challenge, a little voice in my head answers, "I know I can do this." Do you have a mantra? That statement is mine. Like the stray kitty who adopted us, it just came to me. I didn't sit in silence to find it—it has been there all along. I give it space to work, and boom, just like that, it does its mantra magic. Centering me enough to move forward with the internally frightening prospect in my path. Sometimes, it's an important interchange with a patient. Other times, it is starting a new venture or parenting more thoughtfully.

I Know I Can Do This Because I Already Did

I was born with hip dysplasia. It was a gift in disguise. There were surgeries throughout my childhood and adolescence that required body casts and immobility. I learned to walk four times. I have never taken my body for granted in my life. In this way, I had the body of an old person as a child. As I have aged, I watch friends start to have difficulties with their bodies, and to them, it seems like a betrayal.

The space between expectations and reality is where happiness or disappointment lies. When your expectation is set at "Isn't it great I can use these legs?"—everyday activities become celebrations. It's not just gratitude my right hip offered up. What's deeper and mixed in with my ego? A sense that I can do anything. Frankly, being unable to walk really sucks. And yet, I learned how to do it again and again. Through the pain, the being different, the sitting and waiting, acting as the punchline for jokes. Somehow, the crutches or the chair—the parts of me being old—placed me as other, and I was able to enjoy that status. What it told me was that I will not break. In fact, after this downtime, I will be better. It taught me "I know I can do this."

Psychologists like to catalog human behaviors, and one way we assess behavior is with research. We have been studying gender roles for a while now, and we have found that men tend to ascribe their behaviors to these categories: <u>winning, emotional control, risk-taking, violence, dominance, playboy, self-reliance, primacy of work, power over women, disdain for homosexuals [sic], and pursuit of status</u>. Wow. Look at that list. The higher the scores on these scales, the more masculine the man. This is toxic masculinity. It is bad for everyone. Men have their role to play in raising emotionally healthy, more well-rounded sons as well as for branching away from traditional gender roles on their own. But what can we, women, do?

We can look at our own gender roles and take charge of this situation. Here are the categories women ascribe to: <u>nice in relationships, thinness, modesty, domestic, care for children, romantic relationship, sexual fidelity, and invest in appearance</u>. Um. Given all the options in the world, THESE are the ones we want? Some are in direct conflict with the male expectations, and most are in direct conflict with living a full life that will be productive and offer the world 100% of your potential. Take a minute. Evaluate your allegiance to these values. Then take a look at the male ones. There are a few pretty awful behaviors in the male list and then some that women ought to consider.

One of my dreams is for men to be more like women in some ways, and women to be more like men. In other words, gender is a social construct. Psychologists have known for quite a while that gender and sexuality are a hoax, and I am inviting you to the party. Being free from the 'ideal feminine' is my wish for you.

When I was growing up with a bum hip, I was different from my peers. And being different from the start could have gone a lot of ways for me, but luckily (and thanks to my parents), I was not allowed to see it as anything but positive. When you are inside the social world enough to feel loved but not enough to feel the same, you can start to safely see that 'normal' is a lie. For human beings, being outside the social status is a nightmare, and it can even mean death. But when you've securely seen what being different looks like, it can free you to explore new possibilities for yourself without the constraints. And it is lovely.

So, step 1—Separate yourself from the constructed social norms that hold you back. Get some perspective. Take a look at the list of expected gender roles and reconsider how you want to define womanhood for yourself. Hey, redefine manhood while you're at it too because we are all part of this stew.

Being Radically Selfish

When I talk about selfishness, women usually bristle. And I am tired of that. Let's think of selfish as in self first. In my practice, I see most women put others first. Women will sometimes even put what they think another person wants ahead of their own wishes! This will not help anyone. No one wants this.

What do I mean by Radically Selfish? My mantra sums it up: "I know I can do this." This is a fundamentally selfish belief. I know I can do this. What 'this' is—fill in the blank. When I get an idea about who I want to be, what I want to do, what my purpose may be in life, I am free to consider any possibility and to know that if there is pushback, I know I can do this. Thanks, hip.

Radical selfishness means putting yourself and your goals at the center of your world by connecting better with yourself and others, building your confidence, taking control of your thoughts/feelings/actions, and challenging yourself to test and reach new limits. You can help yourself along the path by creating a *Support Scaffolding* (e.g., therapist, friends, mentors, colleagues) to help you reach your goals and to stay on the path you have set out for yourself.

Being radically selfish means trying new things, stepping outside of constraints that do not fit who you are or where you want to go, and also cleaning up your unfinished business. Here's the rub ... being radically selfish does actually add to the betterment of the people near you and to everyone you influence. Think about it, if we all took time to connect better with ourselves and others, follow our dreams, and have power over our thoughts/feelings/actions, I'm guessing we could see some positive changes in the places we are living.

Often when I talk about radical selfishness and goals, people hear: work/being in business/making money. Sure! That's great! But that isn't our whole lives, is it? When I had my tiny babies, I was radically selfish about my time with them. It was often difficult because it interfered with how other people saw motherhood/my career. I wanted to spend lots of quiet time just sitting with them, and my husband and I were lucky enough to make the choice for me to step down making money for a little while. My career and bank account took a hit, and that was a choice I made for myself because of my goals at the time. I owned that choice just as I own the decision to get my doctorate or marry my husband or wear navy blue dresses any chance I get. Large and small, at work and at home, these are all parts of our lives, and they all matter.

Sometimes we have choices to make, and sometimes we have what I like to call 'mini-choices' to make. Mini-choices are within the limits of our lives. Some things take more time than others to move. Systematic   oppression/racism/sexism/heterosexism/transphobia/

physical illness or injury or disability/access to money or other re-sources—these are just a few of the very real barriers that impact our abilities to make choices with a capital C. And we all have boundar-ies. And yet we can still make mini-choices while moving the wall inch by inch. A large part of changing mini-choices to Choices is the people we surround ourselves with, the dreams we allow ourselves to have, and the focus on our goals that we maintain. Being radically selfish can start small. Small ripples can grow to become waves.

Get the support you deserve to move the mountain. And as we move forward, we can create a community of people who lift one another up. But of course, that is in line with one of my main goals—equity and equality for everybody. And we can do this be-cause if we all engage in radical selfishness, we will head toward our goals and shake off the constraints that we allow to mold us into boxes that leave our unique thinking, voices, and contributions in the dust. And that is unacceptable.

I know we can do this.

ABOUT DR. KELLY RABENSTEIN DONOHOE

Dr. Kelly Rabenstein Donohoe is a licensed psychologist. She earned a Master of Science in Applied Developmental Psychology from the University of Pittsburgh, a Master of Arts in Counseling Psychology at Boston College, and a Doctorate of Counseling Psychology at Chatham University. Dr. Donohoe is the creator of the concept FluidEQ. FluidEQ is the ability to make meaningful connections at home, work, and in the world based on awareness + education + empathy.

Dr. Donohoe's interest lies in relationships between people and the ability (or inability) for individuals to deeply connect through interpersonal communication. Dr. Donohoe's research findings (along with co-authors) have appeared in the *Journal of Psychotherapy, The Clinical Psychologist,* and *Urban Education* as well as an edited book, *Bringing Diversity to Feminist Psychology,* and many more. Additionally, she has presented at more than twenty national conferences throughout the world. Dr. Donohoe has a forthcoming book focusing on bringing awareness to bias to promote greater connections in your life.

Dr. Donohoe is currently affiliated with Carnegie Mellon University and Chatham University. With more than two decades of experience, she has worked within a wide range of clinical settings, including hospital in-patient, detention centers, partial programs for children and adolescents with autism spectrum disorders, inner-city schools, private college preparatory schools, college counseling centers, community mental health, community organizing NGOs, and as a consultant for companies who want to improve productivity through increased communication. Dr. Donohoe now helps people and companies prepare for transitions/challenges, change, and grow their productivity.

CHAPTER 4

Waiting for the Weekend

Jennifer Hood

Go to school.

Do well.

Go to college.

Do well.

Get a job.

Do well.

Get married.

Do well.

Don't complain. Work hard. Pay bills. Be an adult. Be an 8–5-er. Work. Pay bills. Work. Pay bills.

That's what's EXPECTED, right? And that's just what I did. In fact, I didn't just do WELL. I Excelled. I double majored and minored in college, graduated, started a job in Corporate America that I quickly moved up in, got married, and together we both quickly moved up in our respective careers and made a shit ton of money.

Then divorce hit—looking back, maybe I SHOULD have expected that. At this point, I was at a loss. *What do I do next?! This certainly wasn't on my agenda. There was no contingency plan for this. No checklist to follow to recover.* So, I did what I knew best. I carried on, threw myself into my career even more. Before I knew it, years had passed by. I was in the cycle of working for the weekend. You know how that is, right? Come Monday, you are already waiting for Friday.

It was five more years before I even took a breath—before I slowed down, stepped back from my life, and looked at where I was. And where I had landed was NOT pretty. I was 10+ years into a career I HATED, that stressed me out, that took all my time with no reward or appreciation, that benefited me in no way but a paycheck. I was in a relationship that was literally destructive—mentally, emotionally, and physically (that's another story, another chapter, another book). I had gained weight, I looked awful, I was tired in all the ways you can be tired. Tired of putting up a front, tired of being the strong one, tired of taking all the crap, tired of fixing everyone else, tired of taking the blame, tired of trying to fix things, tired of working just to pay bills, tired of being TIRED!

On one of the most tiring of days, I learned a simple lesson that I'll never forget. Driving through the tollbooth on the way home from work, I gave my normal smile and said with a sigh, "I can't wait for Friday." The attendant stopped me and said, "Stop wasting your life waiting for the weekend. You're missing out on TODAY."

That little bit of advice followed me around all week. It tugged at my mind, plucked at my heart. I chose to spend some time counting my blessings rather than drowning in my issues. From that moment, without even realizing it, I started making moves toward a better life. I banished the toxic from my life—people, relationships, habits. I embraced the positive. I started taking care of ME. I made sure to make the most of EVERY day and to stop losing ENTIRE WEEKS waiting for Saturday and Sunday. And things fell in place. I was able to support myself, which I hadn't expected. I found love—real, ever-lasting, day-in-day-out, good times and bad times love. And funny thing, what used to be UNEXPECTED started becoming the EX-PECTED. We got engaged and married fairly quickly. No one judged; no one was surprised or shocked. It was so RIGHT; it was expected.

As love replaced unhappiness, I quickly realized I was still not satisfied in my career. But I stayed because it was stable, and frankly, I didn't know what else to do. Good employees just didn't QUIT! There were too many questions, fears, doubts on the other side—what if the grass wasn't always greener?

By the grace of the universe, another opportunity came to me. And certainly NOT mainstream, not expected, not a standard option. But I reflected on all the other leaps of faith I had taken and realized it's when I let go of judgment, expectations, norms that great things happened. So I leaped and have yet to touch the ground!

Just four months after putting faith in myself, I did the REALLY UNTHINKABLE. I wrote out my letter of resignation to my corporate career of 12 years. As my hands shook, my chest tightened, and my breath caught in my throat, I pushed send to EVERY upper manager I had. I sent it to my new VP of less than a month, to her executive assistant, to HR, to my previous supervisors. I went against the age-old adage; I burnt every damn bridge. I knew if I was doing this, I had to do it big, and I had to ensure there was NO going back.

Within minutes, my phone was ablaze. And you know the first statement I heard that solidified my decision 1000%? "Jen … I can't believe this. We never EXPECTED this." Yep. Thank you. Thank YOU for confirming I was on the right path. I'm tired of doing everything just because YOU expect it. I'm tired of being taken for granted because YOU EXPECTED me to just handle it. THANK YOU for taking all the weight off my shoulders.

Even crazier … when I told my closest friends and family what I had done, they weren't surprised! They smirked, love sparkled in their eyes, and they said they were proud of me. Something I thought was totally crazy. They wondered what had taken me so long! I never felt so free. From THAT moment, I learned to live life completely differently. To let go of ALL EXPECTATIONS—of myself, of others, for myself, for others. I learned that there is no blueprint, no checklist of life, no norm or standard. And that when you allow yourself some freedom, some grace, and open yourself up, the opportunities are boundless.

Go to college; don't go to college.

Get married; don't get married.

Have a family; don't want kids.

Work 8 a.m.–5 p.m.; make your own schedule.

There is NO right or wrong. Life ISN'T so black and white. It's a beautiful mess of colors. A kaleidoscope of amazingness and blessings. You just have to open your eyes. I let a CAREER dictate my life for too long because I thought a JOB is what made me valuable. That a JOB and the paycheck it brought was my contribution to a relationship. BUT, at the end of the day, a JOB IS A JOB. And if you hate it, if it benefits you in no way than a paycheck, then you need a new one.

I honestly can't wait for the time when a woman just standing up at work and saying "This isn't for me" is the new norm. And with an HR background and strong personal sense of responsibility, I still feel guilty for saying that! Imagine a world where quitting your three-digit paycheck, with hours and hours of overtime, to go play with turtles is a norm! Where Moms AND Dads work from home, following their passions, to spend time with their little ones. Where someone isn't judged because they aren't married yet, don't have kids yet, or got forbid; they just put themselves first for a little bit.

The only JOB that really matters in LIFE is loving, appreciating, and enjoying every day. Love your career, love your home, love your family, love your friends, love yourself. RESPECT yourself—by doing things you love, by saying goodbye to what you don't love but stay with just because it's EXPECTED. Make the UNEXPECTED the NEW EXPECTED! Don't let anyone else dictate how your life SHOULD GO.

Now, every day is Saturday. Every day is a day to wake up with gratitude. To use the fine china. To celebrate. To LOVE big. It's time for everyone to start LOVING TODAY and stop wasting the week.

ABOUT JENNIFER HOOD

Jennifer Hood lives in Harrison City, PA, with her husband, Jeremiah, and their two fur babies. She is a health and wellness advocate, a domestic abuse survivor, has a one-year-old half-a-million-dollar skin care and cosmetics business, and currently active in her passion by managing a local gym. This is her first publication of what she hopes to be many, as she wants women across the world to feel the freedom to pursue their passions and be comfortable with living outside the mainstream. Her purpose is to "Help women rediscover their self-worth and live the fierce lives they deserve, all in a killer set of heels." You can find her on Facebook under 'Jenny Lynn' as the host of multiple groups dedicated to health and wellness, motivation, positive affirmations, and more.

CHAPTER 5

Who Are You?

Sonali Dutta

The world and so-called society always find a way to draw a line between two individuals. Separating them due to uncontrollable and natural factors such as gender, religion, nationality, so on and so forth. We as individuals are very used to these differences, mainly because we have seen these differences being pointed out rather than our similarities being celebrated.

I am blessed to be born in a family who break the monotony of how society has taught us to think and feel. I was involved in every big and small decision-making and always taught the importance of voicing out opinions. Even then, I was a very timid and weak person in the company of people. Due to my shy and quiet nature, there were many instances where I had to let go of the things and people I held close to my heart. I was that person (still am) who people needed for advice. But deep inside, no one knew I was yearning for someone to lend me their ear.

I tried everything to please them: clothes, friends, education, and sometimes even broke my own heart thinking I could be a part of the 'normal' crew. It took me quite some years to realize that the happiness and peace which I was searching for elsewhere was actually within me. I was the source of my own happiness. I bowed down to the fact that I didn't need to fit in.

My uniqueness lied in the way I conducted myself. The way I spoke, the way I dressed, and the values I held. Thus, a new journey began. I started studying myself and my surroundings. I became more like myself and less like the perfect version which everyone else wanted to see me be. Inside my heart, I had come to terms with the fact that I may have to walk this path alone, as I had no idea how the world would see the 'Real Me.'

Slowly but steadily, things started to take shape. Refusing to change myself, I kept my head held high and saw that more and more people accepted me. As I started to fall in love with myself, so did the world. I was attracting the crowd who resonated with my thinking and letting go of the ones who didn't. Every now and then, I get questions of how and why I changed certain things about myself, and I respond by telling them the truth: life is too short to live as someone you're not.

Once we start to discover ourselves, all questions of life will be auto-filled. We are too busy judging other people and debating how the world should be instead of fixing ourselves. Do not wait for anybody to tell you how you should be living life. What's the fun in spoilers? This is one puzzle that only you need to solve.

Ask yourself, "What makes me happy?" Look at yourself in the mirror; do you love what you see? Forget what they say. Forget what they want. I just want one voice, and that's yours. If the answer is positive, then you're through. **Your battle is to take an oath which states that you will only evolve, not change.** If the answer is negative, then ask, "What?" What is it that you don't like about yourself? Is it something which can be taken care of? Why not give it a try! Be honest with yourself and chalk out a plan which will eventually help you love yourself more.

I believe in the saying, "The World looks at you the way you look at Yourself." If you look at that person in the mirror and feel weak, then that's what you'll be treated as. If you see a strong, confident, and happy person, I cannot wait for you to find out what awaits you at the end of the rainbow. It's all within us. Every mistake we made and every trophy which we've won was because of this one ultimate weapon—Confidence & Self Belief.

If it weren't for that, I would still be living life at the mercy of what others wanted me to be. All your successes, no matter how insignificant it is to the world, should be celebrated. All your mistakes, even if no one's watching, will be the cause of your sleepless nights. We can fool the world but not ourselves. Why not try being true? No harm done, I promise.

That being said, I encourage you to have faith. Everybody has courage; they just need the right motivation. There's no better way of pulling you out of the shell I've also lived in for years. Look around and understand all the things you're losing. I surprise myself EVERY SINGLE DAY. Constantly growing with each passing day, I'm now both the performer and the judge, as I hold the exclusive right to choose when to reward or punish myself.

Every individual has one something or the other which sets them apart. But instead of highlighting that aspect of ours, we take it as a fault. **Being Genuine and Raw is the new cool**, and if you look back into history, it has been that way from the very start. It all comes down to one concluding factor, "**Are you ready to put your real cape on?**"

ABOUT SONALI DUTTA

Sonali Dutta, better known as Sonali the Endless River, is a digital marketer, blogger, and trainer. From early childhood, she knew she was different. Introverted by nature, she has always been a shy observer and listener. Being a curious individual, she has tried out different things just to get a taste of what she liked and what could be taken up as a profession. From tele-calling to designing, operations to marketing, she always had her own creative way, using which she learned her craft.

Soon after being fed up with the way the corporate world worked, Sonali understood that she wanted to do something which would give her the freedom to call her own shots. Learning and observing along the way, she started "The Endless River," a place where she vents out her thoughts for the sole purpose of teaching her peers lessons which life had taught her.

Sonali aims to make her personal brand a globally known platform where topics such as insecurity, shortfalls, struggles, and failures are discussed out in the open. **Build a Community around Kindness and Gratitude which seeks out the truth that Human Beings are more alike than different**. Sonali has made the world her playground by converting communication, which was once her biggest weakness, into her ultimate strength. She now networks with people across the globe, irrespective of nationality, gender, caste, religion, and all those factors by which society differentiates us, to spread her message.

CHAPTER 6

Becoming a Person Who Will Go Far

Olivia Solomon

To an outsider, my young life may seem like a utopia. I live with my middle-class married parents and a younger brother. I attended a thoroughly-funded, well-staffed public school district from kinder-garten until I graduated. I was very involved with school-sanctioned activities, including the swim team, the marching band, and National Honor Society. Just 10 minutes from my house is my mom's side of the family, whom I am very close to. I have many great friends from swimming, band, and my classes at school that will last a lifetime. These activities have led up to me recently beginning my future by attending a top-notch, competitive university in which I'm receiving half-off of my tuition, living right beside the beautiful city of Pitts-burgh.

To someone looking into my personal 'fishbowl,' it looks like I have it made and that my life leading up to this point was nothing but sunshine and rainbows. Of course, this isn't exactly the case. Finding my true work ethic, learning to take leadership in all situa-tions, trying to help my brother through his life, and finding meth-ods to resolve my personal roadblocks are the vital reasons why I am the strong, resilient woman that I'm writing about today.

One of the many important life skills I learned through both my government-funded education and my knowledgeable parents is the importance of a hard work ethic. Starting from when I was old enough to walk and talk, my parents taught me that nothing good comes easy. No, they weren't acting maliciously toward a two-year-old child, but they were trying to instill great values and morals in me and trying to make me the best version of myself. For example, if I didn't eat my vegetables, I wouldn't be allowed dessert. I could only go outside if my room was clean, and I had to finish my homework before I could watch TV. By working hard and following their examples set forth for me, I learned how achievable my biggest dreams and goals were. Although my parents instilled good work ethic and values in me, I did not completely understand the true meaning of those lessons until high school. When I was a freshman, I still believed that I'd still do well by not studying and only putting half of my efforts into my homework and projects, still managing to receive a 90% grade point average for the year. To some people, a low 90 GPA is a cause to celebrate, but in comparison to my friends, I had the lowest. To me, this was a formative moment in my life because I knew that I didn't want to be seen as 'average.' I wanted to make something more of myself.

Because of my new found motivation, I spent my sophomore year ensuring that I understood every math problem in class and all of my homework assignments. I also created Quizlet flashcard sets to study the periodic table of the elements in chemistry, and I spent extra time revising English essays. After I accomplished these tasks that were challenging to me, I realized that extra time and extra effort really made a difference for me, and therefore I knew what it took to succeed in more difficult and challenging coursework. During my junior year of high school, I took Advanced Placement American Government and Politics in addition to taking Advanced Placement Biology in my senior year. Although both of those classes were extremely daunting, it was an eye-opening experience, and I am so grateful that I signed up for both of them. Both classes taught me three things: to find the studying method that works best for me, to work harder than before, and to give me a glimpse into the intense rigor of college classes. Although I always didn't receive the test scores I wanted and lost countless hours of sleep, I am beyond thrilled that I stepped out of my comfort zone and took those classes because they truly taught me about the level of hard work I need give for the rest of my life.

Through my two years of being a section leader in the marching band, I learned valuable aspects of leadership that I would not have learned by blending in. I learned that sometimes I can't be both everyone's friend and a leader. I learned during my junior year that in order to be respected as a female section leader, who is leading people younger, the same age as and older than me, I had to learn to play my best and learn to build relationships with everyone in drumline. My senior year, I actually had more of an opportunity to lead my section, and I felt better about my leadership abilities because I was now confident in my ability to build good relationships with people.

In addition to being a formally titled leader in the band, I gained knowledge about how to take leadership in all situations. From instances as small as doing a little bit of extra work in group projects or by helping others with their jobs once I finished mine. Learning and practicing leadership is a vital reason why I selected my particular major in college.

Helping my 16-year-old brother through his whole life is a huge reason why I'm the woman I am today. When my brother was two years old, he was diagnosed with an autism spectrum disorder. From that moment on, my parents have done the most to help him adjust to life, live with his disorder, and to be able to function on his own without assistance. From when my brother was diagnosed until he was about six years old, my parents had him see so many therapists and participate in every social event he possibly could. From when he was four years old until he was nine, he had a specific TSS spend nearly the whole day with him. The kid has been through hell and back in order to be where he is today and has faced the world with more courage than most people have in their entire lifetime.

With that being said, from the moment he could talk, I would always play school with him in our basement, play computer games with him, and prepare him as much as possible for every new territory he walked into. I taught him about what happened at preschool and kindergarten as well as middle school and high school. I am beyond proud of the young man he is today, functioning perfectly without aid. I believe that me helping him through all of his struggles and helping him adjust to life has made me who I am today and is a huge reason why I selected my college major.

Although helping my brother through his life, the biggest reason why I am the woman I am today is that I had to learn how to get over my own personal bumps in the road. I have struggled with anxiety since the young age of eight, and it has been no easy task. As any normal person doesn't like to be publicly humiliated, I have battled with an irrational fear of being sick in public where everyone can see. What started as a small fear turned into a full-fledged phobia of vomit and any general sickness that people would notice.

This fear started in the third grade when I woke up one morning and just felt like I didn't want to go to school. I felt that school was out of my comfort zone, and my home was safe, where my mom and dad were there to make sure everything was okay. From there, the phobia grew larger. I became, and still am to this day to some degree, a hypochondriac. I thought that the smallest pain in my stomach meant that I was going to get sick, and then my mind would spiral.

I tried seeing multiple therapists to work out my problems by talking to a third party, which ultimately didn't work for me. My parents took me to see multiple doctors to see if something was truly wrong with my stomach, or if it was just all in my head. Turns out I was 100% okay; it was just my fear that constantly plagued all of my thoughts.

Middle school was the hardest part of my life thus far. For that matter, middle school is a hard time in everyone's life. Everyone's going through puberty, and hormones are all over the place. This made my time in middle school harder. I spent so many days in the nurse's office because I made myself feel sick, and when I wasn't in the nurse's office, I was in the guidance office. It was a hard time for me because my body was out of whack, and so was my head at that time.

Once middle school was in the past, I began high school. Of course, my anxiety followed me there. Freshman year was particularly hard. Adjusting to a new school, filled with 1,800 students who were all older than me, was a huge challenge. At this point, my fear had turned into a fear of constantly being watched and judged, so when I had the opportunity, I would sit in the back of the class. During freshman year, I didn't give a single presentation and opted out of the points, no matter how much it costed my grade, because I had anxiety of presenting in front of my peers. Through this year, I still spent many times in the guidance office and at the nurse's. It gave me a melancholy feeling that nobody else felt this way and that I felt alone.

Ninth grade was the year I realized that therapists can't take away how I feel, the guidance counselors can't take away how I feel, even my parents can't take away how I feel. I realized that I am the one who controls how I feel. I was the one who fed into my anxiety over the years, and I am the only one who can flush it out.

Before I knew it, freshman year was over. Although the majority of my anxiety was left in the past since then, I have had some brief relapses but nothing to the extent of the past. Through it all, I learned not to care so much about what others think of me. I came to many realizations that I know the symptoms of being sick and what's real and what I feed myself into. Even as I write about my past with my anxiety, I realize how much progress I have made since then and how much mentally happier I am today.

However, through all of my anxiety and life experiences thus far, I could not have made it through it all without my amazing parents and brother as well as my friends in high school on the swim team and in the band. Even though there would be days that I would cry as I ate my breakfast, dreading going to school to another day of fear and worry, I never wanted to go to cyber school because it would make me feel a sense of giving up, and I would miss seeing my friends every day. I am so grateful for being a part of two awesome programs which showed me what true friendship and fun really is.

As of now, I am currently attending Duquesne University's School of Education to become a Secondary Mathematics teacher, and I'm double majoring to earn a Bachelor of Science in Mathematics as well. I decided my major because it combines two of my favorite things, solving algebra and calculus problems and helping others learn and grow. I hope to shape the minds of others in the future and to help students through what I experienced.

I admit, I know that there will be many mountains to climb in my future. I understand that nothing in life is handed to me. And I understand that I will face problems and accomplishments. However, I am proud of the woman I came to be today, and I can't wait to see all that I will accomplish as the woman who I will become one day.

ABOUT OLIVIA SOLOMON

My name is Olivia Solomon. I am 19 years old, and I am currently a freshman at Duquesne University. I am from Greensburg, Pennsylvania, and (when I'm not at college) I live with my mom, dad, and brother. As mentioned in my story, I previously was very involved at my high school with the swim team and the marching band. Today, I still love to swim for exercise and play music for fun. When I'm not knee-deep in calculus homework or hanging out with my friends, you'll find me playing the ukulele or eating Chipotle.

As of right now, I'm dual majoring, with hopes to get my Bachelor of Science degree in Secondary Mathematics Education and earn a separate Bachelor of Science degree in Mathematics as well. Although college has been a lot of hard work, I have found time to make friends and have fun as well.

Today, I would not be where I am without the constant love and support from my family and friends. My life's been quite the journey thus far, but I'm just getting started.

CHAPTER 7

Success Comes from Trying

Tracey S. Yang

Learning moves us toward success. Persistence and truth are two character traits that need to be learned in order for us to be successful. Below is an explanation of these traits that move us toward success:

Persistence

Persistence is imperative if success is to ever come to existence. We cannot look at past failure as an indicator of us failing in our future endeavors, but instead, they must merely be looked upon as learning tools. It is important to learn from our past mistakes, and then the next step is to continue onward, concentrating on the things we do correctly. Each time we experience a setback, it is essential to look at what occurred adequately, efficiently, honestly, and also rationally. Along with this, it is imperative that we ask ourselves these questions, "What did I do wrong in this situation?" "What did I do right?" Then we must improve upon these occurrences. Self-evaluation prepares us to try again with experience. We find purpose in something that fuels us with intense passion. It is something that gives us the potential for meaning and duty toward our living.

In this way, purpose keeps us motivated, and success comes to existence when moving forward with persistence.

Furthermore, the following personal example demonstrates this perspective: During my first study abroad as an exchange student, I was bullied. The horrifying and agonizing experience of bullying was carried out by the foreigners located at my language school. Due to the stressful environment, my grades declined, and ultimately, I was sent home at the end of the school semester. When discussing my negative experience, being bullied, with the supervisor of the program located there, I was told the following, "I have to look out for the other students. Due to the present information, you cannot return. There are some people who just don't like some people."

After that statement, I decided to look into the possibility of attending another language school the following semester. After much research and a few attempts, I was accepted into a language school located in Tokyo. It is then I tried again. I persisted. During the flight to Tokyo, I happened to sit by a New York Times writer on that plane. We began to converse with each other. By the end of the conversation, he asked me, "Do you want to write for the Japan Times?" I replied, "Yes." From there, we worked out an article for me to write. The New York Times writer ended up writing the article about my personal experience himself instead of me writing it. However, the collaboration was an interesting and fun experience for me.

At the new language school, I experienced a better environment suited for me, and I was included. My grades, once again, picked up to above average, and I did well in the Japanese program. Just think for a moment, what if I had decided to quit after that one negative experience? None of this would have happened. What aspects of your life have you quit too soon? In those negative situations, what can you learn from that experience to help you with your future?

Lies, Lies, and more Lies

Lies are not an accurate representation of who we are as individuals. Without clarity, truth cannot be obtained in us. Lacking clarity allows lies to keep us stagnant in life because clarity is the trait that guides us. However, with truth, we are capable of seeing reality objectively. Truth and clarity give us the opportunity of being able to push past uncomfortable feelings, the lies. By doing so, this action will keep us moving forward. Therefore, I say, for our own benefit, do not believe the lies our inner self tells.

For us to fully flourish, we cannot attach ourselves to the lies that others give us, neither can we believe them. This thought brings one experience to mind. At the age of 20, I met someone I referred to as a friend. Let's call this friend Person B. Person B said to me, "You won't amount to anything in life." He went further to say, "You will never be a leader because you are an introvert." Below is the translated version:

> It is easier for me to hate you than to admit who you really are. I hate that I can no longer control you, so I want to hurt you. Why don't you believe the words I have spoken anymore? Why can I no longer control you? I thought it would be easy for me to control you since you have empathy, love, and kindness. Since I can no longer control you, I want these words to hurt you. It is in this way I can see your strength, but I want you to feel weak. I do not want you to see your strength. I do not want you to see your talent, for those things in you actually exist. I don't want them to be. I don't want you to have them, so I want you to be nothing. It makes me feel bigger when you are so little, weak, and feeble. I have to put others down. I have to put you down. Being who you are makes me uncomfortable. It shows me who I am also, and I can't admit it. In my world, I can be the only one with any form of greatness. I choose to believe this instead. I am afraid that you will make it, so I must stop you. Please, you have to believe my lies. In conclusion and reality, one day I think you have the potential to make it, and I don't want you to.

To summarize what Person B truly meant, he didn't want me to succeed, and he tried to plant doubt. Luckily, a few years after this incident, I was invited to become a member of the National Honor Society of Leadership and Success. Person B's words did not succeed in stopping me from success. As stated by John C. Maxwell, "Leadership is not about titles, positions or flowcharts. It is about one life influencing another." It is true. If you are influencing another, then you are a leader. A title did not define me, nor did membership in the National Honor Society of Leadership and Success. However, the event did greatly impact me, so I humbly accepted their invitation to join. I felt honored.

Are there people in your life who have told you lies? Are you dwelling on these debilitating lies? What lies do you need to let go of? Today is the time to start. Let go of the lies and be the best you. Maybe it is not others who are telling you lies. Maybe it is your inner self telling lies about you. Here is another example: One day, while surfing the internet, I came across a meme with a horse tied to a blue plastic chair. The horse probably outweighed the chair by 1,000 pounds, but he allowed a false mindset to hold him back. The meme stated, "Sometimes the thing that is holding you back is all in your head." How many of you are like the horse and allow a false mindset, implemented by your inner self, to hold you back? Do you say things like "I can never be x, y, and z because I am not x, y, or z"; "I cannot do that because of x, y, or z"; "I don't have a degree in x, y, or z"; or "I am not like him or her"?

Sometimes the thing that is holding you back... ...is all in your head.

Sometimes other people do not need to put us down because we do it to ourselves. While we need to maintain a rooted reality, we must not fall to the illusion that ties us to something smaller than ourselves. Telling yourself to jump off a tall building, believing you will fly, will result in death; however, riding in an airplane gives you the ability to fly by machine. This is problem-solving. What are the plastic chairs, the lies, in your life that are holding you back?

In conclusion, be practical with your goals, but also take calculated risks. Remember to learn from each failure, and do not believe the lies that others and your inner self have stated. Truly, chase after your dreams and also make them a reality.

ABOUT TRACEY S. YANG

Tracey S. Yang is a respected thought leader, business owner, and artist. She uses her life experiences such as her previous chronic illness as examples in her writing in hopes that others can find their own form of greatness. She currently resides in Mid-northern Alabama, USA, alongside her husband, John. Her website is traceysyang.com.

CHAPTER 8

Worthiness from Within

Nicole Jansen

I grew up in a busy entrepreneurial household. My parents loved me and my brother and each other. We were a close family and did everything together. My dad owned an automotive repair and gas station franchise that was open seven days a week, and my mom did the paperwork. My brother inherited my dad's mechanical abilities, so he was always at the shop, cleaning tools and learning the ropes. When I was seven, my parents got involved in a direct selling business, and since it was headquartered in our basement, I offered to help. First, it was opening the weekly shipment of boxes and writing down product orders. By the time I was 14 years old, I was handling a good portion of the paperwork, freeing my mom up to focus on building relationships. My dad wasn't the detail guy. He was gregarious and outgoing—he did all the presentations. It was a lot of fun, and I loved every bit of it.

I was a good student at school, with a natural inclination toward athletics, academics, and music. My parents were very proud of me, and I got along well with the kids at school. Accomplishments came easy for me, so I never thought anything of it. I just did what came naturally to me at the time. I won three of the five awards given out at my grade 6 graduation. It surprised the heck out of me. I had no idea I was doing anything worthy of an award. Therein lay the problem.

Somewhere along the way, I decided that I wasn't worthy. I knew my parents loved me very much; they were just busy. I knew I was a good person, but in school, my two closest friends would shift from being friendly and kind to making fun of me and getting others to make fun of me as well. They said they didn't like that I was so good at sports, winning all the races. Why didn't I want to hang back and have fun with them instead?

At one point, they created a nickname for me, 'Eugene,' from the main character in a movie. Eugene was a super-geek. I wasn't a geek, but they had to find something to get at me. Then one of those friends started pushing me around, trying to get me to fight with her. Nothing happened. I was stronger than her, and she knew it. I brushed her off and walked away. But it stuck with me. My friends couldn't be trusted. My parents were busy with important things. In my child-mind, I deduced that I wasn't worthy of love and attention. I wasn't important.

When I was 16 years old, I started my first official business. I also became very involved in my parents' business and eventually shifted all my focus there and partnered with them in my early 20s. It grew to a $10 million business spanning Canada, USA, and several other countries. I never sought any credit for its success. In fact, I basically worked for free, and it was my choice to do so. I didn't want a paycheck; I was investing in my future. Nothing made me happier than seeing my parents thriving, happy, helping people, and making a difference. Besides, one day I'd inherit it all anyway. No big deal.

Unfortunately, that business ended up falling apart. We lost everything. Financial stability, relationships, and worst of all, confidence and trust in people. My parents never fully recovered from that; however, I managed to extract a ton of lessons and went on to build a successful coaching business. Leave the past in the past; I can handle this.

Fast-forward, I meet the man of my dreams and get married at 38 years old. A little late for a first marriage, some might say, but hey, we were in love, and that's all that mattered. The first few months were wonderful. We were happy together and envisioned a bright future. He was American, so I packed up my business and my home in Toronto (Canada) and moved to California to be with him. At the time, I owned a franchise that I was struggling to make a go of. The franchise system I invested in had major issues, and after four and a half years of pouring my heart into it, I cut my losses and walked away. A month later, my husband announced that he had changed his mind and didn't want to be with me anymore.

Ever been at that point when you throw your hands in the air and say "Really!?!? Is this how it goes???"? I was devastated. "Why me? What did I do to deserve this?" All the un-worthiness that I had harbored from my childhood came up and hit me in the face. "I'm not worthy of love. I'm not pretty enough, not interesting enough, not smart enough. I'm not enough. Who was I to coach others on success? Who would want to listen to me? My own husband didn't want me." 30 years of personal development had given me powerful tools to work with, but this cut deep. I needed something more. I explored topics ranging from inner healing to radical forgiveness, marriage, relationships, soul-purpose, spirituality, feminine-masculine polarity, and pretty much everything in between. I hired coaches who suggested I try different approaches to get him to notice me. Nothing worked. In fact, it just made it worse.

After much soul-searching, studying, praying, reflecting, and piecing things together, I discovered that my worthiness and value came from within. Nobody could give it to me, and nobody could take it away. Like a newborn baby, I am worthy simply because I am. That was very freeing for me. I learned to love myself unconditionally and, in the process, learned to love and forgive my husband unconditionally, despite everything that happened.

Today, worthiness from within allows me to stand strong, no matter what. After my husband left, a business partner left, several clients canceled (two of my largest clients on the same day), and my father and mother both passed away suddenly less than two years apart. There's more, but you get the point. Life happens. Even to this day, I'm dealing with things that stretch my heart capacity. So, how does one develop a sense of worthiness that comes from within?

I'm going to use a model I learned from Tony Robbins when I completed my strategic invention coaching certification through Robbins-Madanes Training (RMT). I've adapted it for my use and teach it now to every person I coach. It's simple and yet so powerful in shifting our experience of life. As Tony says, nothing has meaning except the meaning we give it. If you want to change the way you see yourself, others, and the world around you, you must change your focus, change your words, and change your state.

#1 – Change Your Focus

What are you focusing on? I realized during my self-discovery process that I had been focused on protecting myself, proving to myself and others that I was worthy of love and attention. Then when I was rejected, it all came crashing down. So, I launched a pity party. I'd call my mom and a few close friends, cry out to God, and ask "Why me??"

Certainly, there is a time and place for grieving loss and receiving comfort from friends and family. But that's not a long-term strategy for healing and growth. What you focus on expands. When you focus on feeling unworthy, you will feel more unworthy. When you focus on your worthiness from within—your value that comes simply from being—your subconscious mind goes to work to show you all the ways and reasons why you are worthy and valuable. Whatever you tell it, it will reinforce. And because your subconscious mind doesn't know the difference between what is real or imagined, if you tell it a lie ("I'm not worthy"), through repetition and reinforcement, that lie will become a belief that runs your life. It literally becomes a neuropathway in your brain. The good news is that you can change it. There are several techniques you can use. Here's one of the most effective:

Daily Gratitude – I'm a big believer in expressing gratitude. I thank people all the time and can easily find things to be grateful for in my life. What I discovered, however, is that I wasn't grateful to myself. I'm not alone. Nearly every coaching client I've invited to do a daily gratitude process excludes themselves from the list. They're grateful for their family, friends, job, health, but what about their spirit, resiliency, courage, honesty, kindness ...?

I encourage you to acknowledge yourself daily. Perhaps you've heard the saying, "Recognition: Babies cry for it, and grown men die for it." It's true. We all need to be acknowledged, and the single, most important person you need to receive it from is yourself. Every day, focus on self-qualities to be grateful for. Not in an arrogant "I'm better than other people" fashion; rather, an "I'm grateful for who I am and who I'm becoming" way. Don't wait for someone else to do it for you; do it for yourself.

The added benefit of gratitude is that it also shifts your focus from fear to love, scarcity to abundance, and opens up the possibility for a bright, beautiful future.

#2 – Change Your Words

We talk to ourselves all day every day. Are you speaking confidence and life into your soul, or are you beating yourself up for your shortcomings? The happiest, most joyful people on earth have shortcomings. We all do. The difference is what they say to themselves. If your best friend talked to you the way you talked to yourself, would they still be your friend?

Change your words; change your life. Notice the limiting words you say to yourself, write them down, and then flip them to be more empowering statements. Affirm yourself. Be your own best friend. Write them in the present tense and repeat them until you own them. The key to affirmations being effective is feeling the words, not just saying or thinking them. "I am beautiful." Feel what it feels like to be beautiful. "I am a miracle." Feel what it would feel like to be a miracle.

Your thoughts and words have creative power. What are you choosing to create today?

#3 – Change Your State

The easiest state to change is your physiology. When you're feeling depressed, unworthy, lacking in any area, shift your body. Depressed people slouch. Straighten your posture and look up. Go for a walk and get a change of scenery and some fresh air. Nature is abundant. Reconnect with your true nature, which is abundant. Spend time with people who inspire and uplift you. Sure, sometimes your friends need an encouraging word, and you can be there for them. However, beware of energy vampires. Breathe in love and abundance and breathe out fear and lack.

I hope my story encourages you that if you're feeling unworthy, you're not alone. I've been there and found the path to worthiness that goes far beyond what anyone else says or thinks. It has afforded me a peace that surpasses understanding and the ability to be the calm in the midst of the storm. Believe in yourself. You're worth it!

ABOUT NICOLE JANSEN

Over the past 30 years, Nicole Jansen has coached and trained thousands of people to transform their lives and achieve extraordinary results in business. In her view, there is nothing better than seeing people excel and live their best life, particularly when they are elevating others at the same time.

Applying her unique blend of business mentorship and personal mastery, Nicole's clients not only experience a substantial increase in sales, team performance, and profitability, but they also experience greater confidence, clarity, and personal authenticity through discovering and playing to their strengths.

She is a certified human behavior specialist, business breakthrough coach, strategic intervention coach, and has been personally trained and mentored by some of the top business, sales, and leadership experts in the world. She is the founder of Discover The Edge and the Leaders Of Transformation Podcast & Community.

CHAPTER 9

I Am Not the Same Woman Anymore

Aline Yska

We all have scars ... Life is a learning process; I know that now. The question is, when you face a challenge or a life-changing event, how do you overcome it? Do you stay in a place of sadness, pain, and anger? Do let your negative emotions take control of you, or do you become a better and stronger person? That's what empowerment is about: the process of becoming stronger and more confident.

Divorce—that's what happened to me. I know I am not the only one, and it's not the end of the world, but I thought it was the end of my world ... I thought I was married for life. I never thought I was going to divorce one day. My life was all planned. I got married at 22 years old. Yes, that is very young, but I thought love was enough to jump into the married life. I don't regret it for a second because I have three beautiful children, and I am so grateful for them. I experienced love, even if I got hurt in the end. I gave my all to this marriage. Maybe my all was too much ...

The truth is, I lost myself in this marriage. I was happy when he was happy. I am a very positive person in essence, and for 20 years, I tried to be the perfect wife, the perfect mother, but it was never enough. I felt I was not good enough. The problem is, when you put your happiness in someone else's hand, when your happiness depends on someone else's happiness, it's very shaky.

Happiness has to come from within; it's an inside job. I became emotionally dependent on my ex-husband. I felt like whatever I was doing, it was never the right way to do it. I was doubting myself all the time. Year after year, I tried to be up to somebody else's expectations of me. It was always my fault. I was always blamed when things didn't go the way they were supposed to. I was criticized about the way I looked, the weight from the pregnancies, the way I talked, what I was saying, and so much more ... At the end of my marriage, I thought I was not capable of doing anything by myself. I was not myself anymore. I was trying to be what he wanted me to be.

I accepted being treated that way for a long time. I took responsibility, and I didn't blame anybody for it. But how long can you accept verbal and emotional abuse? How long can you let someone put you down until you don't know who you are anymore? Well, I did it for 20 years until I couldn't live like that anymore. When you let someone disrespect you, you neither respect nor value yourself. Even though I still loved him, the relationship became toxic for me. I was suffocating, and I had to breathe again.

I was so scared to get divorced. I was hiding to cry for months so my children wouldn't see me. My self-esteem was below zero. I thought I couldn't live by myself, and the idea of being a single mother was terrifying me. I had to take control of my life.

Finally, one day, I hit rock bottom, and I decided it was enough. I had to find myself again. I was not happy anymore. I thought marriage was happiness. I was wrong. For many years (too many), I tried to be who I was 'supposed' to be, not who I really am. I decided to take my life back, and I promised myself no one in the world would tell me who to be. I just wanted to be me, perfectly imperfect. I wanted to make my own decisions, even if I had to mess up sometimes. I set myself free, and I finally got divorced, but I didn't know who I was anymore. I had to rebuild myself and find my purpose.

One day, a friend of mine told me about an intensive seminar about positive thinking. I signed up, and this seminar transformed my life! What I learned was amazing, and I felt like the Universe was sending me messages and the support I needed to climb the mountains step by step. I learned how to let go of my fears and my negative emotions. I had no more anger nor resentment in my heart. I could breathe again. I also learned how important it was to forgive the ones who hurt you and to forgive yourself. I finally learned to love myself without anybody's approval. My transformational journey had begun.

During the divorce process, I went to therapy. I was like a bird with a broken wing trying to fly again. As I got stronger working on my self-development, I wanted to use my story and experience to help others. I always loved helping. Back then in France, where I was born and raised, I went to University and had my bachelor's degree in Psychology.

As I was searching for what I really wanted to do in my life to be happy (besides being a mother), I heard about life coaching. I remember the day it just hit me: *That's it! I want to be a life coach. That's how I am going to help others and use my story in a positive way. Maybe I went through this for a reason … I want to help people believe in themselves and be who they want to be. I want to bring more happiness in other people's lives and see them happy!*

So, I went back to school and became a Transformational & Empowerment life coach. I found my purpose: share my message and help others empower themselves the way I did for myself. As I was sitting in the classroom during my training, I remember thinking: I am exactly where I am supposed to be! It all made sense to me. I was learning the tools to transform people's lives for the better, and I was feeling amazing. I couldn't stop learning and discovered the power of positive thinking and NLP (Neuro-Linguistic Programming). These techniques were just mind-blowing to help unblock negative emotions from the unconscious mind. I saw my fellow students having a breakthrough during the training, and to be honest, so did I. As I was working on my personal development, I was also learning how to help others. It was so empowering. I felt like a dove flying in the sky. When I was done with my training, and my coach called my name to hand me my certification, tears of joy and accomplishment rolled down my eyes. That was my first victory!

My divorce was hard on me. I went through very difficult times, but today, I am not the same woman anymore. I lost 40 pounds, and I feel better about myself physically. I moved out of the big house where I was living to a smaller apartment with my three children. I love my new place; it doesn't matter the size, but we sing and dance whenever we want.

Today, I know who I am. I feel free to be myself. I am not perfect. (Who is?) But I rediscovered myself. I love this quote: "You never know how strong you are until being strong is your only choice" (Bob Marley).

I accomplished things I thought I would never be capable of. I am a single mother of three amazing children; I am doing it, and I am not scared anymore. I am a professional life coach, and I love it. I coach women from all over the world. I am who I am: MYSELF. I found myself again, a better version of me: a strong and confident woman.

I will never forget the day my 17-year-old daughter told me, "Mom, I am so proud of you. You are the strongest person in the world. You work so hard and accomplished so much!" That day, I knew I was doing something right. It meant the world to me. That was the best victory ever. I had shown my children everything is possible when you put your mind into it. They are the reason why I am fighting every day, and I didn't give up.

I am writing this chapter today to share my message. It took me time to realize what happiness is: you have to be happy by yourself, for yourself. We all deserve to be happy. Love yourself enough to never depend on anyone else emotionally. Distance yourself from negativity and toxic people. It is not easy to be positive every day, and life is not a fairy tale, but you can have the life you want. The first step is to decide and then make the change you need.

Another lesson I learned is to never apologize for being yourself. You are good enough and worthy; don't let anybody tell you otherwise. Reach out for your stars to accomplish what you want. I wanted to be a life coach, and I did it! What do you want to do that will fulfill you? Don't be scared to dream big and make it happen because when you will empower yourself and set yourself free from what is holding you back, you will have the life you want. Enjoy each step of the way. "There is no path to happiness: happiness is the path" (Buddha).

Every challenge we go through is part of who we are. We learn from our challenges and become stronger. We all have scars; they are part of us. It's up to you to either let the pain take over or climb the mountain and empower yourself. Love yourself for who you are and believe in you. Don't let your negative thoughts take control of you but, instead, take control of your life, your thoughts, your emotions, and be yourself.

I realized that confidence is the key to happiness. Life is too short to be unhappy. If you are looking for happiness outside of you, you will keep looking forever. I thought I couldn't survive my divorce, but I found the power within myself to overcome my challenge. Find the power in you because it's there; we all have this light that shines and wants to become a burning fire. Even if change is scary because you don't know what is next, and you have to get out of your comfort zone, don't let your fears paralyze you. You are the master of your life, and you create your own story.

I am not the same woman anymore. I am an empowered woman, and if I did it, so can you!

Love and Positivity.
Aline Yska.

ABOUT ALINE YSKA

Aline Yska was born in Paris, France. She graduated in Psychology from University Paris 5 (UP5). She moved to Miami, Florida, with her family 15 years ago. She is a single mother of three amazing children. She is a Transformational & Empowerment life coach specialized in women empowerment, relationships, and divorce recovery. This is her first publication. She shares her messages each day on her Facebook group Positive Mindset Transformation. You can follow her on Facebook under 'Aline Yska' and her business page NEW START LIFE COACH. She was interviewed on a French TV channel about the benefits of coaching and the cultural difference between coaching in the USA and Europe. She coaches women all over the world and has a passion for helping others be the best version of themselves. She is a master in Positive Thinking Psychology and a Neuro-Linguistic Programming practitioner. She helps her students let go of the negative emotions that are holding them back so they can take control of their lives in a positive way, be stronger, more confident, and be happy.

Empowering Words

by Empowered Women

"Never interrupt someone doing what you said couldn't be done."

–Amelia Earhart

"God puts people in our life at just the right time to let us know that He has a plan and we have a purpose."

–Mary Dreliszak

"It is our choices that show what we truly are, far more than our abilities."

–J. K. Rowling

"Optimism is the faith that leads to achievement."

–Helen Keller

"Make the most of yourself by fanning the tiny, inner sparks of possibility into flames of achievement."

–Golda Meir

"Life is a continuous string of moments, it should be a priority to enjoy as many moments as we can, while we're able to."

– Tasha L. Bradley

"I define leadership as having three parts: first is seeing what needs to be done to make things better or seeing a problem that needs fixing; second is having the vision, the skill, and the wherewithal to change the system; and third is the most important task of mobilizing the energy of others to organize and act in ways to achieve that vision."
–Susan J. Herman, 101 Great Quotes From Successful Women Leaders

"We're here for a reason. I believe a bit of the reason is to throw little torches out to lead people through the dark."
–Whoopi Goldberg

"A good leader inspires people to have confidence in the leader; a great leader inspires people to have confidence in themselves."
–Eleanor Roosevelt

"Forget about the fast lane. If you really want to fly, just harness your power to your passion."
–Oprah Winfrey

"You have got to do the right thing even if it is painful. Don't trim or track all over the place. Set your course and take the difficult decisions—because that is what needs to be done."
–Margaret Thatcher

"Nothing will work unless you do." *–Maya Angelou*
"If you don't like the road you're walking, start paving another one."
–Dolly Parton

"A strong woman is a woman determined to do something others are determined not be done." *–Marge Piercy*

"You don't have to be anything but yourself to be worthy."

–Tarana Burke

"Everyone needs to be valued. Everyone has the potential to give something back."

–Princess Diana

"I alone cannot change the world, but I can cast a stone across the waters to create many ripples."

–Mother Teresa

CHAPTER 10

Unleashing Your Inner Superwoman

Charlotte Lee Bowman, aka Charlotte (Char) Murphy

My intentions in this chapter are to ***inspire, empower, and motivate you*** in and through my words and my life's journey to finding, unleashing, rediscovering, or reinventing the 'superwoman' which lies within.

This is written as a gift from my heart to you. Receive and accept it. You will witness firsthand how to not just simply survive but how to thrive being your authentic self, experiencing your wildest dreams and greatest passions, regardless of the roadblocks and detours, enjoying the celebrations and successes along the way. Learn how to maneuver through it all, always moving forward ... landing upright on your feet with a smile on your face, your arms open wide to embrace and be grateful for whatever awaits you. ***Run with it on your unique path ... we call life!*** Fully blossom into who you are and simply BE the best possible YOU that you are capable of being ... ***live you!***

Although it is true, this chapter is about my life experiences, my sacred journey; moreover, it's written for and about you! It is my life's passion and greatest desire to share a sample of my personal and professional trials, tribulations, and successes open-heartedly with love, transparency, encouragement, and a real understanding of whatever you are going through now or already have experienced.

Be that an illness in yourself or a loved one, loss, grief, depression, divorce, abuse, self-doubt ... and in general, brokenness, confusion on what to do, which way to turn next. All of which I have endured, learned, and grown from. I am revealing specific parts of my journey to you here, which I feel will serve you best to identify with my life's examples; to equip you with *the tools; to gain knowledge, wisdom, understanding, and the insight necessary to live the life of **your dreams.***

My journey continues. My goals are to constantly strive with strength, determination, and courage to always move forward, never looking back, taking with me lessons from the past. I have spent years re-educating, re-creating myself, finding something to be positive and grateful about every moment. To do what makes me happy, to live my own dreams and passions. Not what anyone else wants or expects or tries to mold me into. At the end of the day ... to just *live and BE me!* **All of this ... to help you do it too!**

Quoting from *The Wizard's Mirror* by Gari Gold Kennedy, I was struck by a phrase that was very profound for me: "It's about the process, not about the product." In fact, the end result will take care of itself. During the series of 'supernatural' or 'synchronistic' events and occurrences that produce change and spiritual development, we tend to get caught up in the past or in the future and forget to enjoy the process. **That is the key to life.**

I began to understand what it means to truly live these teachings. As in, there are no accidents in this life. And therefore, it is by no coincidence that you are reading these words right now. So, tighten your seatbelt ... ready, set, *LET'S GO!*

Together, let's take a closer look at the title of this chapter:

Unleashing Your Inner Superwoman.

What does that really mean to you? If you don't know, that's okay. Keep reading because I'm going to spell it all out for you right here and now.

You are *stronger,* more *powerful,* capable of more *success*; more *beautiful*, more *loved* than you now know or can even imagine. Yes, YOU! Even if you have had success in your life in many areas that you have accomplished on your own, you already own the strength within to conquer and overcome any obstacles in your path to more. Some of you are just starting out, and that is great! What greater time than now to pick up and learn to stretch and mold yourself into not only knowing who you are but what your passions and dreams for your future life are and to become that person?

Most of us females, even as women in today's society, are taught *not* to think about how unique, special, wonderful, loving, strong, resilient, smart, creative, and truly beautiful we really are. At least that is how I grew up. I am living now in this moment to tell you that it is perfectly acceptable, healthy, if not mandatory, to recognize, embrace, and be thankful for and love all those great gifts and attributes about yourself that you already possess right now. Know that you can accomplish anything you set your mind to. However, the real question is, how badly do you want it? And that's up to only you. Be *patient* with yourself, *love* yourself, *believe* in yourself. *Trust* and have *faith* in the process of becoming you. Always remember, it usually doesn't happen overnight.

Take time to walk through the fields of your life, stopping frequently to pick and savor the fragrant blossoms along the way. Please hear me, sometimes it's not easy to *believe* those things are true or to fully acknowledge and embrace them *in yourself* and realize your full potential. Maybe you even have to have the famous "fake it til ya make it" type of mentality. Soon it will become a **knowing** deep inside your heart and soul. So rooted into your being that no one can ever take it from you. *Own that one!*

Let me regress a bit into my journey, my story through life up to this point. Yes, I have been depressed, anxious, scared, alone, lonely, lost, confused, and questioning every single thing about my life. Sometimes even asking myself: *Why am I here? Who AM I? What should I do now? How can I be of greater service? How can I honor myself, my family, and help others at the same time?*

I AM real. I get it. I know what you are going through. From the top of my head to the tips of my toes, I know. I have felt like giving up; I have felt like it's not worth it; I have felt and believed I'm not worthy, not good enough, not pretty enough. At my absolute lowest point in life, the actual breaking point of totally giving up, was when it finally hit me. And all of those questions finally started changing into the realization of who I AM and literally why I had been saved repeatedly from the clutches of abuse, serious illnesses, bitter heartache, mass confusion, depression, and even death.

From the time I came into this crazy, beautiful world, innocent and pure, the learning began. I grew up in a highly abusive home. Both physically and mentally. I witnessed and experienced it unto myself and the other members of my immediate family. It was not pretty. There were times I literally thought I was going to die right then, in the midst of a battle. Or if not me, one of my family members. Thankfully and by the grace of God, we were spared. However, now bravely bearing throughout life the heavy emotional and mental scarring and learning how to cope with these memories that were stuck somewhere deep inside, it is not easy to dig deep to forgive and move on. That subject of forgiveness has its own chapter in my upcoming book. I only mention it briefly.

I was taught that *I can do anything I want to do if I set my mind to it, set goals, work hard, get a solid education, and sacrifice what I had to.* This is something I have passed on to my son and he is passing on to his children. For those things, I am grateful and have long since forgiven my parents.

I now know that education is important but can and does come in many different forms. I have experienced almost all of them. I went to college, quit after three years, got married for all the wrong reasons at age 21 in search of 'something else.' Someone, something to take care of me. I didn't know better ... that's not why you get married!

I had recently learned that my father was dying of ALS, a disease better known as *Lou Gehrig's Disease*. I was a *daddy's girl*, despite the abuse. I was told that he had maybe five years to live, and it would be a slow, horrid, painful death. My family would not only go through this, but we were his caretakers for most of those years. It was brutally difficult, as well as heartbreaking, to watch my strong, fearless father, only 54 years old when he died, to suffer such a loathsome and debilitating death without dignity. I was horrified, again scarred with these painful memories for the rest of my life.

I had my only child at age 22, a mere child myself. Out of this failed marriage came one of the greatest gifts of my life, if not the greatest! I had no clue as to what I was doing or how to raise a child, much less one who would grow up to be one of the best people I know with a huge heart, successful in his own right ... one of the most loving fathers and husbands there can possibly be.

The tests and lessons came hard and fast, and I was unprepared mentally, physically, emotionally, and spiritually. But through it all, we became the best of friends. We literally *raised each other* going through it all together, just he and I. He has taught me some of my greatest lessons. I'm so proud and grateful for him.

My son was two years old when my father died. I was newly divorced, alone for the first time in my life, except for my beautiful child, with *no support* to get through it all. I had quit school, and I was totally in the spin cycle. I was financially broke and totally lost.

I soon returned to college and received my bachelor's degrees, sadly leaving my son every day with strangers and paying for school with student loans and working part-time to help with living expenses, groceries, and daycare. That great lesson I was taught from a young age kicked into high gear. *I knew I could do anything I wanted to do if I wanted it bad enough and was willing to work hard for it.*

After graduating from college, I worked different sales jobs for eight years until my son was ten. **I started questioning who I really wanted to be; asking, who am I now?** The sales profession was not fulfilling for me, but it paid the bills. I had for many years wanted to be an attorney. I wanted to *help people*. I wondered, *How in the world would I continue to raise my son alone and afford to go to law school?* I dug in my heels, decided somehow I could and would make it work, and began *the process*. I prayerfully turned in the application, and I, a single mom at age 32 amongst 80 mainly recent college graduates still living at home and supported by their parents, was admitted to law school. It was a very joyful moment in my life. However, it would become a grueling three years of sacrifice, the most intense long hours and days of reading and studying I had ever done. I very soon began to wonder if I had made a mistake, but there was no turning back.

As a full-time day student, I struggled daily to provide for my young son, to be both Mom and Dad, while striving to make the grades. I *was determined and wanted it bad enough. My mind was focused and set.* I did what I had to do and graduated with honors.

I started focusing on passing the bar exam and getting a job. Could I do this after all? What if I didn't pass? And then, God forbid, what if I couldn't find a job? I used every tool and resource I had learned from all of my life experiences and did both. Another milestone accomplished! *I believed in myself first and foremost. I didn't give up; I had faith and persevered.* All of the grueling work; the blood, sweat, and tears; the many sacrifices would soon pay off.

I went on to become a successful attorney with a thriving law practice. Everything was going great, and I received the honor of being voted "Best Lawyer in Central Arkansas" after 13 years of practicing law. Suddenly, shockingly, out of nowhere, in the very same year and month, after receiving that award, the seemingly impossible occurred. After all I had overcome and survived to get to that point in my life, I was diagnosed, the first time, during a routine mammogram, with **Breast Cancer**. A totally disturbing, completely shocking revelation. I was blindsighted, to say the least. When the radiologist who read my test results sat me down to give me this news as I sat there in alarmed disbelief, he looked at me and said, "You look like a deer in headlights." I can still hear those words as they burned into my brain.

I had a Lumpectomy, and radiation for 60 straight days while still trying to work and keep the balls in the air. And incredibly, I was diagnosed with *three additional illnesses* over the next eight years with recurrent **Breast Cancer**. I can't even tell you how many biopsies, procedures, tests, all kinds of surgeries (including a bi-lateral mastectomy and reconstruction), I have had. I ended up losing everything—my career, my identity, my home, my business, and ultimately the love of my life (we married shortly after the first diagnosis) ... everything gone. *I was blessed, with my life spared again and my son. Again, living strong, faithful, fearlessly unyielding, and positive through it all ... I had to.* And I am grateful for every bit of it.

You see, if it wasn't for all of those circumstances, I could not be sharing my success story to empower and inspire you now. I am **gifted** to be a **survivor**. I was born that way, **exactly like you**. I am thriving, despite everything; more determined than ever, continuing to reach and achieve my greatest goals, living my passions, my authentic self, *UNLEASHING MY OWN INNER SUPERWOMAN. And you can too!*

The biggest lessons for all of us are and always will be to love, be kind to and believe in yourself. Know in the core of your being that you can and will do and be whatever your heart desires. YOU are a strong and power-filled woman; you already have what it takes! Dig deep inside to find her. No one else can do it for you.

*Live your truth, your dreams, your authentic self with faith and determination. **Never give up.** Watch yourself learn, grow, and bloom into your real self ... who you have been all along ... though maybe hidden through life's misfortunes, mysteries, defeats, setbacks, and confusion.*

Ask yourself these questions: Who AM I? What are my greatest dreams and aspirations? Am I living my authentic self? **What can I do now to put myself on track to be all I was put here to be?**

Here are words I still live by every single day from the great motivational speaker and teacher Dale Carnegie, in his best-selling book How to Win Friends and Influence People:

"If you think you can't, you won't.

If you think you might, you might.
If you think you WILL, you WILL!"

Congratulations, for the seeds are now planted. All you have to do is water them and watch them grow! *Now* is the time. Put your tool belt on and nail it! Go kick some ass and show the world the real **YOU!**

ABOUT CHARLOTTE MURPHY, ATTORNEY

Charlotte Murphy is a graduate of the University of Arkansas, Little Rock, with BS degrees in both Psychology and English. She received her Juris Doctorate Degree from the University of Arkansas School of Law, Little Rock, with honors. She practiced law in Little Rock for 15 years. Her law firm was Murphy's Law.

Charlotte Murphy retired from law as a four-time breast cancer survivor to pursue other passionate lifetime goals such as motivational speaker and writer, personal and professional life coaching, freelance art, acting, and beaching it. She is an entrepreneur and loves creating new business through research, marketing, and coming up with new ways and ideas for doing things. She has done business consulting and jury analysis, helping other attorneys pick the best jurists for their particular case.

Charlotte's interests and deepest desires in life are to teach, inspire, encourage, and motivate women of all ages through the transitional stages of their journey. That could be through illness, family issues, traumatic situations which they may be feeling lost and no hope for, or helping them start their own businesses. She also has a heart for volunteer work with charitable foundations such as breast cancer, ALS, and Alzheimer's diseases. She is an animal lover and rescuer. Gratitude, integrity, honesty, love, honor, and charity are her guiding principles.

The greatest success in Charlotte's life, no doubt, has been to raise her most kind, loving, giving, fun, smart, and successful son. He has become the best husband and father to her two beautiful grandchildren anyone could ever dream of having. Charlotte's life is a dedication to them.

CHAPTER 11

"Log Kya Kahenge?" ("What Will People Think?")

Sarika Bhakta, CDE

As a South Asian woman living in today's America, I have faced a myriad of challenges, especially as a first-generation immigrant from India. How do you embrace one's traditional South Asian culture that is the bedrock of collectivism (focus on the group) while struggling to integrate with the American culture that is rooted in the notion of individualism (focus on the self)? This can be extremely daunting, exhausting, and detrimental at times, both physically and psychologically. The guilt, the obligation, the expectations, the sacrifice all in the NAME of one's community to save FACE in one's community. "**Log kya kahenge?**" A common Hindi phrase which is mirrored and echoed in all corners of the world that tends to paralyze women from feeling empowered and living their full potential. "**What will people think?**" This continuous cultural tug-of-war pressed on my heart. Making choices impacting my life for the collective good of what others thought and felt.

> "Do you know how much your parents have sacrificed for you to be here in America?"
> "Good Indian girls stay away from dating, drinking, and desires."

"You must learn to cook, clean, and care for your home and family. We are training you for your future husband and in-laws."

Your experiences may be vastly different than mine. What connects us, especially as women, is having tendencies to primarily put our family, work, and community first, oftentimes at our own expense. This spans all cultures! Serving others, taking care of loved ones, and having a sense of duty are great traits to possess, yet we need to have self-preservation.

"It's okay to love someone. It's okay to love yourself more."
–Anonymous

"Refuse to be ruled by how others see you. The only thing that matters is how you see yourself."
–Anonymous

My grandma Bhikhiben was inspired by Mahatma Gandhi to become a freedom fighter to liberate her fellow Indians from the political and social oppression they endured under the British colonial rule. She was only 16 and the only girl from her village in Gujarat, India, standing up for her convictions in the face of adversity. I always felt I embodied her spirit, her drive, her tenacity.

For a very long time, this very spirit, drive, and tenacity felt broken ... I was lost. Personally, I was spiraling out of control, getting further away from my true core to the point that I didn't even recognize who was looking back at me from the mirror anymore. Many times, pursuing my own dreams, aspirations, wants, and desires felt inherently wrong, as I have been ingrained with familial, societal, and cultural biases. Biases that were patriarchally dominated and disapprovingly screamed out loud that it was selfish for me as a woman to focus on myself, as, for centuries, women around the world have been treated as second-class citizens.

In a span of six years, my ego took a beating due to three rejections from three different organizations to be considered their top executive. In all three cases, they hired someone who was a tall, white male executive.

The last interview changed the trajectory of my life. I felt elated and confident about my skills and qualifications. I was interviewing with leaders who personally knew my successful track record, having worked with me closely in the community. At the start of the interview, someone immediately commented, "Well, you know we really wanted Jay (name changed) for this position. He, of course, is unavailable."

One week later, I was watching the news when, all of a sudden, I heard the newscaster congratulating and interviewing the new executive that was hired for the position which I had literally interviewed for. I was stunned. What was going on?! I was still waiting to hear from the Search Committee, so I thought I was still in the running. *SHOCK. HURT. PAIN. BELITTLED.* I was finding out at the same time the rest of the world was, that the position was filled by someone else. Tears started to course down uncontrollably, primal screams coming out of my body of their own volition. They ended up hiring a tall, white male executive ... someone who looked like them. Two hours later, I received an email from the Search Committee. Two hours too late.

I realized I needed to be more self-centric and authentically make decisions, assess relationships, and create opportunities that helped my core be in equilibrium. I had to re-shift my focus from worrying about "Log kya kahenge?" ("What will people think?") to start asking myself first, "What do I think?" By honestly exploring who I was internally, I began to trust the choices I made. It helped lessen the depression, anger, anxiety, and guilt that I was carrying, as I felt emancipated to live under my terms versus living someone else's version of what my life should be.

In a span of 3 weeks, as an Asian immigrant woman from India living in today's America, I took a detour in pursuit of the allusive American Dream and established my own consulting firm. I redefined what success and happiness meant for me and what I want my legacy to be. *I am creating a BETTER new normal for me.* Financial independence is crucial for all women to have. Yet we need to ensure that success and happiness is defined beyond monetary gains. It is how we use our time, talents, and resources to make a lasting impact on humanity for the better.

> "When opportunity knocks, say 'yes' to stretch your comfort zone."
>
> – *Sarika Bhakta*

> "If you do what you always did, you will get what you always got."
>
> – *Anonymous*

As I reflect on some of the greatest achievements that empowered me, it was simply because somebody asked me, and I said yes.

Operating five different entities in my early 20s under one umbrella in Washington, D.C., because William Pierce, my mentor and founding President & CEO of the National Council For Adoption, believed in my entrepreneurial spirit and asked me to join him on his journey. **YES!**

Becoming the Chief Operations Officer of an American Red Cross regional chapter because the Executive Director, Angela Jordan, witnessed my authentic leadership skills and asked me to help impact change. **YES!**

Co-authoring this empowerment anthology book because Amy Waninger, founder of Lead at Any Level, valued my diverse perspective and asked me to collaborate on this exciting initiative. **YES!**

When others notice your dynamic talent, that is a compliment. They have faith and confidence in your abilities; hence knocked on your door. When you say yes, this is the ideal time to "**stretch your comfort zone.**" Place one foot outside your comfort zone and KEEP IT OUT, as this allows a new comfort zone to be formed. All the opportunities that I said yes to above made me nervous, anxious, and scared. Looking back, I realize that meant that I simply cared and was truly invested in the outcome. Identify the opportunities that will challenge you while fulfilling your purpose during this juncture in your life and immerse yourself fully in it. ***Hear you roar; see you soar!***

> "When you release expectations, you are free to enjoy things for what they are instead of what you think they should be."
>
> *–Mandy Hale*

"I expected better from you because you are my best friend."

"I expected better from you because we raised you with Indian values, and love can come after marriage."

"I expected better from you because you are my supervisor, and you should have had my back."

Think back to a time when you had expectations and shared that with someone or a situation occurred that triggered this thought. How did you feel? We need to manage our expectations better. We can only control what we have control over—our own actions and reactions. ***Once we start shifting our perspective on expectations, this will align much closer to the realistic outcomes, lessening the disappointments surrounding our expectations.*** As my nine-year-old daughter, Keya, says many times when she sees something being blown out of proportion, "Drama ... drama. Mr. Llama." The smallest inconsequential things start tearing into us, impacting our relationships, as doubt sets in, and trust starts to deteriorate. Suddenly, a molehill becomes a mountain. I heard this somewhere, and it's a great quick mental exercise that I do regularly to put things into perspective while providing immediate clarity. When something is bothering me, I ask myself these three questions:

1. "Will this matter today?"
2. "Will this matter next week?"
3. "Will this matter next year?"

Why borrow extra stress and hurt relationships for something that, in the grand scheme of your life, can remain a molehill?

With that said, I am also a firm believer in "**Blessing and Releasing**" relationships that are negative, one-sided, toxic, etc. In your lifetime, on your journey, you will meet many people. Some will stay with you as you take detours, some will part ways, and some you will have to proactively bless and release from your life. As a very young girl, I moved around from state to state as my parents looked for a place we could call home in America. Unfortunately, when I was of school age, I had to separate from my parents and live with 'loved' ones, at whose hands I experienced a myriad of things that have deeply haunted me. I was powerless to defend myself, let alone stand up for myself or do anything to change the situation. It impacted my self-esteem, my self-worth, and as an Indian immigrant girl growing up in a predominantly white America, I already had identity issues, as the kids were cruel and unaccepting. I learned to bless and release, especially loved ones.

Only you can determine your self-worth and value. Only you can give others the power to have more control over your emotions, thoughts, and decisions. So, let it be your choice to be in control to determine who you want to have alongside you on your life's journey, what role they play, and for how long. This will be one of the most challenging things you do, yet necessary for self-preservation.

As I reflect on my journey thus far, embracing certain traits of being both a traditional and modern Indian woman is my pillar of strength for my core. It emboldens me to be resilient in the face of adversity. It emboldens me to explore exciting adventures. It emboldens me to have faith in the power of positivity by avoiding negative words like no, but, can't, unable, however, etc., which are omitted in this entire chapter. I am following in my grandma's footsteps of being a change agent for humanity and blazing forward without worrying about "Log kya kahenge?" (What will people think?)

ABOUT SARIKA BHAKTA, CDE:
PRESIDENT OF NIKEYA DIVERSITY CONSULTING

A certified diversity executive (CDE), visionary leader, and entrepreneur, Bhakta was born in Gujarat, India, and raised in the American Midwest. Adjusting to the American culture was extremely challenging for Bhakta, inspiring her life's mission of helping people identify their authentic self to be change agents and leaders in today's ever-changing global economy. She has over 20 years of experience empowering diverse talent and population groups to maximize their potential while increasing their cultural competency and global perspective.

Bhakta is a seasoned and multi-faceted executive with expertise in leadership management, strategic planning, talent attraction/retention, resource acquisition, program design/delivery, community/economic development, and parking management. She is a sought-after consultant, speaker, trainer, and community engager due to her high energy, interactive, and inspiring style. In each presentation, she brings the diversity pendulum back into balance in a positive, refreshing, and authentic perspective, affirming everyone is diverse. She transforms organizational cultures enterprise-wide by utilizing Equity, Diversity, Inclusion & Engagement business solutions driving innovation and sustainable outcomes.

Bhakta is also a co-investigator/research collaborator for a national study assessing women's leadership progression in the workplace while conducting a deeper exploration of challenges and opportunities impacting Asian women's leadership trajectory. She is a social entrepreneur, recipient of Corridor Business Journal's Forty Under 40 award, and actively engaged in her region—serving on numerous boards and organizations. She received her Bachelor of Arts in

Liberal Arts & Sciences at the University of Illinois, Urbana-Champaign, and resides in Cedar Rapids, IA, with her husband and two children.

CHAPTER 12

How I Rekindled My Spark and Ignited My Flame of Empowerment

Lynnis Woods-Mullins, CHC, CLC, CPI

Isn't it amazing how we learn the same life lessons over and over again but in different ways?

When we were in our teens, we learned to feel a bit empowered (although we were still scared of EVERYTHING). We started driving, perhaps voted for the first time, or went away to college.

In our twenties, we learned to feel a bit more empowered. We finished college or got married, started that first real job, or had a child.

In our thirties, we learned to feel even more empowered. We climbed the corporate ladder or perhaps bought that first house. We sent our children to their first school experience. We branched into our true womanhood.

Then suddenly, we are in our forties, and we wonder, *WHAT HAPPENED? How did time go so quickly? What happened to our dreams? Where did our motivation and inspiration go? Where is that spark that ignited our flame of empowerment? Where was our motivation, clarity, and focus that propelled us to success? How does one get that spark and flame of empowerment back?* These are the questions I asked myself when I turned 50.

I was at the peak of my career. I had the so-called 'American Dream.' The wonderful husband, four beautiful daughters all in high school doing well, a beautiful home … a great life. Yet something was missing. Even though on the surface it appeared that I had this great life, I felt empty inside. I felt hopeless, lost, and so frustrated at myself for feeling this way. I mean, who does this? How dare I feel unhappy when everything on the surface says I should be feeling grateful and happy for the life I had?

I didn't know who to tell about how I felt. I tried to tell one friend of mine, and I will never forget her response: "Girl, are you crazy?? I wish I had your life. You don't know what problems are. You are just spoiled and ungrateful. Look around. You have it good. Stop whining, girl. You are just in menopause!" *Just in menopause? Really?* Well, it was true; I was approaching menopause. But I wasn't approaching menopause at 35 when I first started feeling this way. I wasn't in menopause when sometimes that feeling of sadness, emptiness, and anxiety crept up on me. No, this wasn't menopause; this was something else. But my girlfriend was right; I needed to quit it! Stop being sad, cheer up, and get on with life.

If only it were that simple. It took an event to wake me up and to figure out what was wrong. I woke up one morning and couldn't stop crying. I felt incredible sadness and anxiety. For the first time in my 25-year career in Human Resources, I totally disconnected myself (turned off both cell phones, pages; unplugged the computer; unplugged the landline) and cried. So much so that I didn't hear the doorbell ring. I finally heard someone knocking on my patio door. It was one of my daughters home from school. She was shocked to see me so upset. I tried to make light of it, but she wouldn't let it go. I don't remember this, but she told me later that I said I just wanted to die, that I was tired of feeling empty. This scared my daughter; she had NEVER seen me this way before. I had always hidden how I was feeling, especially from my children.

My daughter called my husband and the police. Yes, a bit overkill with the police, but when I look back, I am grateful. The police took me to Emergency at the hospital. By this time, I had regained some of my composure but not enough to fool the doctors, counselors, and psychologist I talked to. They all told me I was first of all exhausted and sleep deprived. (How could that be? I slept three to four hours a night. Yeah, right!) They also told me that I was anemic, underweight, and had an anxiety disorder with borderline depression. WHAT??? I knew immediately that now was not the time for my famous denial; now was the time for me to do something about the way I was feeling. For the first time in a very long time, I was beginning to feel a small tingle of hope, of empowerment.

Arrangements were made for me to go on a respite. It was a house, a group home for women who were recovering from trauma. I came to quickly find out that I was not nearly as traumatized as some of the other patients there, but I definitely was in the right place because I had suffered trauma; I just didn't think about it that way.

At the respite, I finally dealt with the death of my mother when I was 31. I had just had my third child. The last time I saw my mom, she was on her way to work, and I told her I would call her that evening. Later that morning, I received a call from my dad saying she had been in a car accident and to go to the family home to wait for him to return home. The baby and I went back to my family home. I felt scared. I wanted to call someone to sit with me while I waited for my dad. I had left my organizer at my house (no cellphone in those days), so I called my mom's office to ask her secretary to go through her Rolodex to get the numbers of some of my friends. I was so nervous I couldn't remember any numbers. I can still hear the secretary's voice in my head and the words she said that would change my life forever. "Oh, Lynnis, I guess you would want to have someone come to be with you. I'll get those numbers. We are so, so, sorry; we all loved your mother so much."

LOVED? LOVED? I said, "You mean she is gone?" That was how I found out that my mother was dead. She was killed by a firetruck on her way to work. I was devastated.

After that, I decided that no matter what, I would never be surprised again. I would do whatever it took to control the outcome. I would try to control my husband, children, my dad, sisters, people at work; heck, I would try to control the weather. I decided to do whatever it took to not have that hurt again. Hence my anxiety disorder and the reason it was so important to take this time at the respite.

At the respite, I could only bring my journal. No books were allowed, with the exception of those books already there. While their book collection was somewhat sparse for my tastes, there was one book there that really resonated with me. It was a book written by Melody Battie, *The Language of Letting Go.* Reading this book and doing the daily meditations opened a new perspective for me. As I prepared to leave the respite, I decided for the first time in many years to take some time off for me. After I left the respite, I took a year's sabbatical to explore what I wanted to do when I grew up. Just the thought of being true to what really motivated and inspired me was empowering.

At the end of that year, I knew what I had to do. I took the leap of faith and decided to pursue what I thought was my true calling. I was ready to make the changes necessary in my life so that I could get empowered to create a life that resonated with me. It was at that time PraiseWorks Health and Wellness was born. PraiseWorks Health and Wellness is a mind-body-spirit virtual wellness company for women over 40.

As I embarked on my journey of creating a life I love, I realized that I needed to keep feeding my flame of empowerment. It is not easy starting a company from scratch, in an industry that is new, using skills I didn't have yet, in a genre that was groundbreaking. Yet I persisted because of these five things I did every day to keep myself grounded and empowered. To keep the flame of empowerment going, I reminded myself to keep these five things in mind:

- *Embrace* the changes in my body, mind, and spirit brought on by growing older and celebrate them. Honor my body even more by feeding it with fresh fruits and veggies, lots of water, and movement.

- *Implement* the practice of Letting Go and Letting God … no more wasting my time with worry. Instead, approach challenges and obstacles as detours to where God wants me to be.

- *Allow* clarity, peace, and joy to be my focus and mantra.

- Recognize the wisdom I have been blessed with and USE IT. SHARE IT.

- *Forgive* those who have wronged me, hurt me, betrayed me … and most importantly, forgive myself.

Continuing to do these five things now that I am in my 60s reminds me that empowerment never leaves me; it just gets hidden for a bit. For it is within my passion that I can find the spark which ultimately lights the flame to my empowerment and to a life of purpose and ultimate joy.

ABOUT LYNNIS WOODS-MULLINS, CHC, CLC, CPI

Lynnis Woods-Mullins, CHC, CLC, CPI, is a certified holistic living and wellness expert and certified life coach for women over 40 and founder of PraiseWorks Health and Wellness—a faith-based mind-body-spirit wellness company that specializes in educating women 40 and over on wellness. Lynnis's company educates women over 40 about wellness through coaching programs, e-books, DVDs, radio programs, webinars, a digital magazine, and podcast programs/video series. The focus topics are educating women about holistic practices, fitness, nutrition, and spiritual renewal.

Prior to Lynnis entering the world of wellness, she was a successful human resource executive for a large HMO. She attended undergrad at Spelman College. In 2009, Lynnis decided it was time for a change and, at the age of 51, started PraiseWorks Health and Wellness.

Lynnis has over 40 years' experience in dance and is an accomplished praise dancer. She is also accomplished in Yoga and Pilates. Lynnis is the host and producer of "The Wellness Journey-LIVE!" "The Wellness Woman Show," and her newest live show on YouTube "Living Well Woman – Holistic Living and Wellness For Sisters." Her shows are heard on iHeartRadio, iTunes, PodBean, Spreaker, YouTube, Self Discovery Network, and over 100 FM radio stations.

Lynnis is the publisher and editor-in-chief of the digital magazine Wellness Woman 40 and Beyond, Different Background ... Same Journey, a mind-body-spirit e-magazine for women over 40. Lynnis is co-author and editor of DeStress The Mess-Minimizing the Impact of Stress on Your Body, Maximizing the Joy in Your Life collaborative e-book. Lynnis signature coaching program is "DeStress The Mess," a holistic stress reduction program that is now available as a virtual self-directed teaching program also entitled "DeStress The Mess." She has recently launched Total Wellness Transformation, a wellness and virtual weight release program.

Lynnis has been recognized as a health advocate for women and has received national and regional awards for her work. She was recently a finalist for WEGO Health Advocacy Award. Lynnis's company was also recognized as Visionary Business of the Year by the National Association of Women Businesses Owners. Lynnis also writes for several blogs and is a featured columnist for Women's Voices E-Magazine, Sacramento Observer Empowerment Series, Post40Blogger, Hive Health Media, and Curejoy.com. For almost 10 years, Lynnis has done countless radio shows, speaking engagements, and has appeared in print media throughout the United States.

Lynnis is married and the proud mother of four grown daughters and three grandchildren.

Social Media Links and Website:

Website – www.wellnesswoman40.com

Podcast - The Wellness Journey Podcast Series - https://self-discoveryradiotv.com/2015/10/21/new-wellness-journey-show/

CHAPTER 13

Learning to Be Bold

Amy C. Waninger

I was interviewing for a promotion within a Fortune 100 company, and I'd gotten to the final stages of the selection process. After a long day of interviews with senior managers, I found myself sitting across from the hiring manager, Ted, a senior vice president with a corner office.

"What did you think of George and Pam?" Ted asked of the other interviewers.

"They have very different approaches to their work," I said, trying my best to be diplomatic. "George strikes me as very creative, while Pam seems to be more methodical. They have different opinions about what this position is and how it should be handled."

My answer must have been satisfactory. Ted moved on to some small talk and then asked if I had any questions for him. I inquired about his boss, whom I had not met, and how her leadership style influenced him. I followed with some questions about travel requirements and other odds and ends. Then Ted asked me, "Is there anything else about you that I need to consider while we make our final selection?"

I decided to put all my cards on the table. "Yes, I believe there is." I took a deep breath. "In an earlier interview, you asked if I'd ever managed a support team or an implementation team. I haven't. You asked if I knew anything about your customers' business processes or the technology your group provides. I don't. You asked if I've ever managed other managers. I haven't. So, I think it's only fair to tell you why I'm confident I can do this job, despite having none of the obvious qualifications."

Ted chuckled, so I pressed on.

"When I started courses for my Computer Science degree, I didn't even know what computer programming was. But I learned how to do it. Once I started working as a software developer, I had to learn a new programming language about every six months. Every project was managed differently, and I had to learn to adapt. My position has been eliminated at half a dozen companies over the last twelve years, each time requiring me to figure out how to fit in somewhere new and learn a new business or industry. Along the way, I've learned how to manage individuals and teams, international teams, teams in matrixed organizations, virtual teams, and teams that were completely dysfunctional.

"I've learned how to design software, rather than build it. I've learned how to translate business processes into automated systems. I've learned how to navigate office politics and big-company bureaucracy. I've learned other parts of the business, other roles, other systems, other technologies, other job functions. Nobody was born with the knowledge to do those jobs. And no one was born with the knowledge to do the position you're seeking to fill. If someone has to learn how to do this job anyway, why not me? I have a consistent track record of learning new things, and that's all any new job is."

Ted nodded slightly, without giving anything away. A bit more small talk, and his administrative assistant knocked on his door. It was time for his next meeting and time for me to go. On the flight home, I worried that I had just talked my way out of the job.

Two weeks later, I got the offer. I resolved to live up to my bold assertion that I could learn to do anything. I approached the job as a child might: asking ridiculous questions, confident in my ability to solve an unsolvable problem, generating ideas without an understanding of what was impossible. I put one foot in front of the other, only looking far enough ahead to keep my balance. I spent the first two months asking questions, taking notes, building relationships, and contributing very little along the way.

My findings were astonishing. We had a unique customer support process for each system we supported ... and there were 35 systems! I decided that the only way to improve my team's performance was to create a single process for everyone to follow. We would leverage an existing help desk with centralized tools as the customers' entry point, calling on our own team members for only the most complex issues. We would have to train the help desk team on our common issues. We would have to train 10,000 customers on the new process. We would have to train our team and our business partners to use the centralized tool. We would have to document everything. And we would have to do it *thirty-five times.*

When the time came for me to present my plan to the rest of the management team, I was literally shaking. I took a deep breath and laid out my approach in detail. My voice cracked a few times, and I prayed no one else noticed. No one mentioned my nerves, but they had all kinds of things to say about the direction I proposed for my team. My plan was audacious. It wouldn't work. No one would agree to it. I was going to fail. I responded with data about the current state, anecdotes from business partners about their pain points, success stories from others who had accomplished what I proposed. "Give me 90 days to show you it can be done," I said.

In the next 60 days, we delivered on our proof of concept. In the 18 months that followed, we replicated the process more than 50 times using templates and tools from the original effort. With a team of 18, we ran as many as 35 concurrent 'process transformation' projects, all while we were taking on more core responsibilities. We cross-trained our team members, and we even trained interns to manage the projects.

The results? The team reduced customer wait times by more than

90 percent. We fixed problems in minutes or hours, rather than days or weeks. Half of our team members received promotions into other groups, and we had become so efficient that we didn't need to replace them. We saved the company $1 million in the first two years alone, which resulted in a President's award for one of our managers. I cited the success of this and other projects to secure another promotion shortly thereafter.

Don't let me fool you. I made a lot of mistakes along the way. My decisions weren't always popular, even when they were right. My decisions weren't always right, even when they were popular. I missed some opportunities to build key relationships. I failed to learn aspects of the business that might have opened new doors for me. There were times I needed help extracting my foot from my mouth because I didn't understand my audience or didn't know what I was talking about. All these mistakes were part of the learning process. So, while I'm not proud of every step along the way, I am grateful for the journey.

I learned so much during this time, but the most important lessons I learned were not related to the business problems, the technology, or the office politics:

1. The ability to learn is a valuable skill all by itself. When you think you need to know everything to get started, you're likely to get overwhelmed. Where would you even begin? Even if you did know everything, your knowledge would quickly become obsolete. Guess what? No one knows everything, and you won't either. Here's the one thing all experts know that you don't: they're still learning too.

2. Admit what you don't know. Ask questions. Thank others for sharing what they know. Collect the knowledge and contributions of others as if they were pieces to a puzzle. When you don't know anything, take it upon yourself to put the puzzle together. Not only will you build your own expertise rapidly, but you'll also be contributing something no one else has.

3. Don't be afraid to be bold. If you need to take a deep breath

and make the case for yourself, do it. I've recently made a point of announcing to a friend when "I'm going to be bold" or when "I've just made a bold move." The announcement invariably serves as a milestone for when good things start to happen.

Following these steps has taken me to some amazing places, both personally and professionally. I've launched my own business where I work with organizations who want to develop inclusive and adaptable future leaders, and with early- to mid-career professionals who want to lead effectively at any level. I've published my first book and am already working concurrently on my second and third books. I've spoken internationally on leadership topics such as Diversity & Inclusion and Change Management.

There is so much more for me to learn. There are countless opportunities for me to take a deep breath and make a bold move. No one was born with this knowledge or these opportunities. If someone has to learn, it might as well be me. And if I can do it, so can you.

ABOUT AMY C. WANINGER

Amy C. Waninger works with organizations who want to develop tomorrow's leaders to be more inclusive and adaptable, and with early- to mid-career professionals who want to lead effectively at any level. She is the CEO of Lead at Any Level LLC and author of *Network Beyond Bias: Making Diversity a Competitive Advantage for Your Career.*

Amy is a professional member of National Speakers Association and a Prosci Certified Change Practitioner. Her other credentials include two degrees from Indiana University and a World's Best Mom coffee mug.

CHAPTER 14

Living My Best Life

Cherie Faus-Smith

My husband and I just celebrated our 17th wedding anniversary. It's a very special day for me and quite the milestone. Between the ages of sixteen and thirty, I found myself in three separate abusive relationships. I had become accustomed to being let down by men in my life, so to finally find a man who cherished and loved me unconditionally was magical.

Feeling nostalgic, I looked through our photo album while sitting on our bed alone. As I flipped through the album ever so slowly, reliving those moments, I came across one of my favorite pictures before we said: "I do."

He looked dapper in his fuchsia short sleeved shirt, gray bowtie, and matching gray vest. His arms were crossed in front of him, and his smile was as a wide as the ocean. He exuded joy!

My five-year-old son, to my ex-husband, was the ring bearer and stood to the left of him. The two of them bonded the day they met, and he wanted to mirror my soon-to-be husband's outfit. They looked adorable. As I stared at that photo, I began to cry. A teardrop plopped onto the photo, but thankfully, it was protected and didn't get ruined. The emotions that I felt surprised me.

After eighteen years of being together and nineteen years post abuse, I thought for sure that I had dealt with the pain. It made me think that perhaps survivors never truly get over the abuse but instead push those feelings deep down inside and pretend to have it all together. And then bam, out of the blue, something triggers us and causes a waterfall of emotions.

I'm grateful to the person who snapped that photo because it is a reminder to me that when we got married, he was truly in love with me, and when I have my breakdowns, which happens occasionally, I can find comfort in knowing he chose to love me forever, despite my flaws.

~

When we first met, I was a broken woman with very little self-esteem and confidence. I could have won an Emmy for my performances, though. He never knew the pain that I was feeling nor the struggles that I was battling from the abuse I had endured for years.

We began communicating via email because we used an online dating website. My family and friends thought I was crazy, especially since it wasn't the "thing to do" in the year 2000. They worried that I could potentially meet a sinister person. But for me, it was perfect. I could hide behind the computer screen and get to know him without sitting face to face. And if he decided that I wasn't the person for him, it made it easier to walk away.

In the beginning of conversing, we asked each other questions. For instance, do you prefer hamburgers or pizza? Or, what was your favorite vacation spot? But over time, he wanted to know more about me. Nothing wrong with that, right?

I shared bits and pieces about my divorce but didn't elaborate on the abuse. It was embarrassing, and it was easier to pretend it never happened than deal with the questions he may ask.

Luckily for me, he was patient. He took things slow, and it was exactly what I needed. Little by little, I opened up about my past but always had a fear that I would somehow spook him, and he would walk away.

We met in person a few months after our first online conversation, and I was over-the-moon thrilled to be finally meeting this mystery man who had stolen my heart.

I'm not a punctual person, but for that date, I made sure to be on time. I parked in the front of the restaurant, and as I opened the door, he was standing there with his hand stretched out for me to hold and step out of my vehicle. Whoa! What a gentleman.

Our conversation during dinner flowed, and I laughed many times. After dinner, we each drove our vehicles to a bar across the street so we could continue our date. We were there for maybe an hour, and I let him know it was time for me to head back home.

He was cool with it and walked me to my car. I stood there for a moment, waiting to see if he would kiss me, and then it happened! He pulled me close to his body, placed his hand between my shoulder blades, and kissed me ever so gently. It didn't last very long, but the passion and energy that exuded from that one kiss was incredible.

We said our goodbyes, and later that night, I took a chance and called him. I hoped it wasn't too forward, but I just didn't want the day to end. Our conversation lasted for hours.

~

After a few months of dating, we decided it was time for him to meet my son, and it was an instant connection. They built Legos on our family room floor, threw baseball in our backyard common area, and watched cartoons. I was relieved but remained cautious.

During that first year, I battled a lot of demons. My insecurities got the best of me, and I began making up stories in my mind. I'm not good enough for him. He'll eventually abuse me just like the others. He's cheating.

The longer I dwelled on those negative thoughts, the easier it was for me to walk away. I didn't want to give up on our relationship, but it was very easy for me to give up on myself. Thankfully, his love was stronger.

A few months after we moved in together, he proposed. As we

planned our wedding, which was a few months after our engagement, those pesky negative thoughts entered my mind again. As hard as I fought to keep them at bay, they still found their way to the forefront.

I never shared my fears with him; instead, I just stuffed those feelings deep down inside, which led to depression and anxiety. A few years into our marriage, I began having anxious thoughts daily, and it came to a head when, in the middle of the night, I had a major panic attack.

My husband called 911, and after taking my vitals, they informed me that it wasn't anything serious. Just a panic attack.

"What the hell is that?" I asked.

The EMT laughed and said, "It's when your brain misfires, causing anxious thoughts and then mimics a heart attack."

Oh great, I thought. Even though they informed me that there wasn't a need to be transported to the hospital, I insisted they take me. My husband and son followed them to the hospital, and after a few hours of waiting in the ER, they let me know that indeed it was a panic attack. The doctor asked my husband if I could quit my job because I was on the verge of a breakdown.

We were a two-income family, but even though he knew it would make things tight, he responded, "Yes, she can quit."

I was released early in the morning, and after dropping me off, my husband left for work. As soon as he walked out the door, I began feeling anxious all over again. The days were long, and I began having trouble sleeping at night for fear I would have another panic attack.

Eventually, I saw a therapist and was diagnosed with a panic disorder with agoraphobia. The worst feeling in the world is not feeling comfortable leaving your house. I hated being stuck inside every day, all day. It felt like I was in jail.

I decided to take control of my life, so I purchased an anxiety workbook and began working through the exercises. My first goal was to leave my house and walk down the driveway to our mailbox. The first time I attempted it, I wasn't successful. My hands shook, my heart raced, and the sweat dripped down my back. But I continued working through the obstacles and my fears. Even though I will always suffer from this mental illness, I no longer allow it to control me.

~

Our marriage survived that hardship, and things were great until my son noticed a weird mole on my back. I, of course, ignored him. And then my husband mentioned it to me and freaked me out.

I made an appointment with my dermatologist, and after taking a biopsy, she called two weeks later to inform me that I had melanoma.

My husband was at band practice when I received the call, and he immediately came home to comfort me. As we sat on the sofa, with my head on his chest, bawling my eyes out, he said, "It's going to be okay." I felt safe and loved but at the same time scared and overwhelmed.

Surgery was scheduled two weeks later, and while sitting in the surgeon's office a few days before, he looked at us and said, "You do realize that people die every day from this cancer."

Stunned and shocked, I turned to look at my husband, and he had tears in his eyes. In that moment, I realized that this man loved me unconditionally. For the first twelve years of our marriage, I questioned his love for me. After that day, I embrace every moment we have together and cherish our love.

The pivotal moment in my marriage was a few years ago when I said to my husband, "Thank you for saving me."

He looked at me and responded, "I didn't save you. You saved yourself."

I've thought about that conversation many times through the years, and he was right. I survived abusive relationships, I survived cancer, and am not allowing my anxiety to beat me. It was time to stand up to my fears, believe in myself, and live my best life. And that's exactly what I'm doing.

I've become an advocate and work with women who are victims and survivors of domestic abuse/violence; I've learned the art of burlesque and pole exercise at a local dance studio; and to celebrate turning fifty, I created a blog named "Feisty Fifties." I'll be sharing my adventures and challenging myself to go outside of my comfort zone in hopes to inspire and empower women to live their best lives and challenge themselves.

ABOUT CHERIE FAUS-SMITH

Speaker, mentor, and author Cherie Faus-Smith is a beacon for victims of domestic abuse. She shines a light on survivors and illuminates a path of prevention toward healthy relationships with an end goal of helping them recognize the signs of abuse.

With over three decades of real-life experiences, Cherie shares that there is hope after abuse. Her open heart has a way of bringing out the best in others.

Cherie's book The Cycle Ended: Saying Goodbye to Domestic Abuse details the struggles in her past abusive relationships and how she found love after breaking the cycle of choosing unhealthy relationships.

www.cheriefaus-smith.com

www.feistyfifties.com

CHAPTER 15

My Life's Journey and Lessons

Jonamay Lambert

"Dignity of human nature requires that we must face the storms of life."

–Mahatma Gandhi

A fond friend of mine has always called me the 'Unsinkable Molly Brown,' and I consider it quite accurate. When I look back on my life, I sometimes think I should have been Job, the Bible figure that endured challenge after challenge. In Greek mythology, Sisyphus is also an example of perseverance and resiliency. Both characters represent what is needed to stay focused on achieving whatever goals one may have.

The DNA I was born with, combined with life circumstances and choices I made, afforded me the opportunity to develop perseverance and resiliency. My journey began at the age of nine, when my parents were in an auto crash that took my father's life and left my mother disabled. My three younger sisters and I were uprooted from our suburban lifestyle and transplanted to a small rural community in southcentral Indiana, my mother's hometown.

As a result of one incident, the car accident, my family life was altered forever. For me, it meant assuming a parenting role to my three younger sisters and my mom. This was one of the early experiences that provided the opportunity and necessity to develop patience, persistence, and an unsinkable spirit.

One of the first lessons I acquired was: *I should take care of others before taking care of myself.* To do that, I developed the ability to block my emotions; my needs were not important. From the fourth grade until I graduated from high school, we moved back and forth five times to the small town of 1,200 people. Each time we moved away, I thought it to be a new and better beginning. I was wrong. While many people thought of me as the girl next door with no problems, that couldn't have been further from the truth. I led a bifurcated life. Some may call that a split personality. *I call it adaptability.*

Making Lemonade out of Lemons

Surviving childhood was a major accomplishment from which I gained many skills. These early painful experiences helped me develop the tolerance, tenacity, and resiliency to get through the many trials still to come. My true test came when I turned 50 years old. During a five-year period, I faced four of the five major life stressors:

- Divorce
- Moving
- Major illness or injury
- Job loss

If I had not been prepared early on to deal with the onset of so many challenging situations, I would probably be full of anger and pain. I don't believe I would have been equipped to withstand all of the stressors that seem to come at one time. Here are some of the things that helped me endure them and, with time, come out stronger:

Adaptability

While I did not have a 'normal' childhood and was forced to

grow up before my time, moving many times and changing schools often contributed to my ability to quickly adapt to new people, places, and things.

Responsibility

The ultimate responsibility of actions lies within oneself. I learned choices lead to outcomes—positive and negative—and at the end of the day, the buck stopped with me. Knowing there was no one to 'bail me out' if I demonstrated poor judgment, I tended to be more careful about my decisions.

Fake It till You Make It or Act as if …

In a small community, it's easy to be labeled and be treated 'different.' Normal in our small town was very much like what we saw on television shows like "Leave it to Beaver," "Father Knows Best," and even the "Flintstones." All three presented the family unit where two heterosexual parents were present, Dad worked, Mom stayed home, the house was clean, laundry done, and dinner on the table at 5:00 p.m. That was a good portrayal of the life we were living before our father passed on. As a result, when I first entered the workplace in my late 20s, I didn't have a lot of confidence. However, I was lucky to have had a wise mentor. One good piece of advice she gave me was to think and act like the person I want to be until it becomes a natural part of who I am. She was right!

Risk-taking

Most of the risks I took growing up were not positive and often created more trouble for me. However, I still consider myself somewhat of a risk taker. I started my business in my mid-20s with no clients and no budget. Thirty years later, I am glad I did so. Life can be too short to walk on eggshells all the time.

Think Before You Act

A close friend helped me understand I was not from a 'privileged' family with connections or money to "bail them out." So, I realized making the right, thoughtful decisions are critical to success. My grandmother often shared the proverb, "A bird in hand is worth two in the bush."

To Thine Own Self Be True

Being in business can be both rewarding and scary. Whenever I have made decisions out of fear, they have resulted in painful, learning consequences. Depending on someone else to make choices due to fear of making the wrong choice is limiting and gives away my power.

While some events in my life have been extremely tough, they have contributed to the person I am today. In closing, I would share that regardless of the challenges in my path, I always held a strong belief that things happen for reasons we don't usually understand at the time or even ever. I have learned what works for me is to cautiously plan for the future but live in the present and say the Serenity Prayer often.

"Don't wait for the storms of your life to pass. Learn to dance in the rain."

–*Steve Rizzo*

ABOUT JONAMAY LAMBERT

Jonamay (Joni) Lambert,
Founder and CEO of Jonamay Lambert & Associates

With 30 years of experience, Jonamay has engaged with a broad range of industries in the Fortune 500, 100, and many of the Top 50 companies recognized by Diversity, Inc. Her mission is to ensure every person has the opportunity to contribute fully and feels valued, respected, and heard.

Jonamay Lambert & Associates focuses on Diversity, Equity &

Inclusion, Leadership Development, and Culture Change services. As an established thought leader in DEI, she has partnered with other firms and organizations to create unique products and services. Some of her previous and current clients include Allstate, Sara Lee, CNA, State Farm, WellPoint, PNC, S&P, Sears, Baxter, SourceAmerica, OneAmerica, and University of Michigan.

She is the author of 13 Diversity & Inclusion Trainer books. Ms. Lambert has been featured in Diversity Inc., quoted by the media, and has presented at national and international conferences.

Jonamay is a partner of Spectra Diversity and co-creator of Spectra Diversity and Inclusion Profile®. Spectra's mission, to honor differences and help others create a diverse and inclusive workforce, is very much aligned with Ms. Lambert's personal and professional values.

She has been a faculty member of the Summer Institute of Intercultural Communication and is a certified administrator and coach of the Intercultural Development Inventory (IDI)®. Jonamay holds an MA in Counseling Psychology and is a certified coach.

CHAPTER 16

The Woman Behind the Bitch Face: Transforming Cultural Norms to Live Our Leadership Potential

Jeanny Chai

I had resting bitch face before resting bitch face was popular. As early as 3rd grade, I remember kids at school would ask, "What's wrong?" and I would annoyedly answer, "I'm fine," while the feeling of emptiness and numbness stung inside of me.

Things at home were chaotic, and I didn't like being the only Asian American in an entire school of white students and being unable to talk to anybody about my true feelings. But I knew that maintaining my perfect little Chinese student facade was what was expected of me, and to air any of my family's 'dirty laundry' would equate to treason.

My family always pretended that we were the perfect little family, never sharing with our aunts and uncles, our neighbors, our friends what was REALLY going on. Facebook in the Flesh, when Mark Zuckerberg was still in diapers. Before we attended parties, my parents and I would be parked in a friend's driveway, arguing and complaining to each other. I remember watching the adult attendees all putting on their smiles before walking into the party, laughing at the right times, and bragging humbly about their children's latest straight-A report cards or acceptance to some elite private school.

My birthday fell on the yearly Taiwanese-American potluck in Naperville, Illinois, on the day after Christmas—it was THE event of the year, the potluck, not my birthday. The celebration of my birth was never spoken of because, heck, my parents didn't even celebrate their birthdays growing up.

At home, my mom would constantly sigh when I was sick and needed care. She would tell me that the most obedient thing I could do is 'not trouble her.' At a young age, I learned not to bother my mom unless my crisis had reached the point as my having an open wound with the risk of fainting from excessive blood loss.

The only time I got attention was when I brought my report card home. A good report (straight As) meant that I was given the privilege of attention from both my father and my mother independently. I craved this time, as it made me feel alive and that I mattered. A bad report (all As and one B) also meant attention from both of my parents, though not the kind of attention I needed or desired.

Early on, I came to live for the words 'good job.' In the moments that those words fell from my mom's or dad's mouth, my beaten-up self-image would take a momentary vacation from the continuous stream of self-criticism and self-loathing. I had learned that my value was to bring my family glory (to never, ever shame them).

The reason we moved to the United States in 1972 was so that I could have a better life and become a doctor. Of course, my parents also made it very clear that they weren't ready to have kids when I was conceived and that I was almost aborted. Oh, and they had wanted a boy. His name was to be I-Chong. Since they couldn't have any more children, I was to be the token boy-substitute-future doc-tor-child.

This may very well have been the explanation for my growing up mowing the lawn, playing with toy guns, doing hours of yard work, learning to put bait on my own fish-hooks, and doing my best to ex-cel in math (which, contrary to popular belief, was not second nature to me). After all, the least I could do to make up for being an inconvenient baby, and a girl, was to do everything my parents wanted, right? I would become a doctor because that was their dream and their plan for me.

Now you probably see how I really couldn't help but walk around with resting bitch face. All this was normal day-to-day living for me. My Asian face was but a reflection of great unhappiness stemming from crushing expectations, emotional restraint, and shame-based child-rearing principles dating back to dear old esteemed Confucius.

All those times that schoolmates have asked me "What's wrong?" I wanted to be honest and say: "I'm unhappy. I don't feel loved or wanted. I feel like I have to keep performing and achieving to make up for the guilt of being born a daughter. I feel like a big inconvenience to my parents every time I ask for something, like help with a school project, going trick-or-treating, seeing the fireworks on Fourth of July, or worse, asking for a birthday present. And I'm resentful that I was forced to quit cross-country, volleyball, and cheerleading (to make time for homework) because that destroyed my efforts to break out of the Asian math-nerd label and perpetuated my resting bitch face."

What Is Your Face Saying?

None of us should ever have to live restraining, shaming, and aiming for constant unobtainable expectations of perfection. Yet, without exception, every Asian American/Canadian/Brit I speak with confirms this cultural norm. We don't even realize we've been Asian-culture-normed. AND, even worse, we don't realize there's the possibility of choosing to transform such suppressing cultural norms, and so, by default, these soul-crushing expectations follow us into every aspect of our adult lives.

As my elementary resting bitch face grew into angry teenager face and matured into a depressed adult face, I still convinced myself everything was 'fine.' I just had to be a better mom, a better wife, and a better career woman ... and then everything would be fine.

It wasn't fine. Not even close ... yet I kept pushing through (yes, you know exactly what I'm talking about, don't you?) until the day I couldn't lie to myself anymore.

In the midst of a painful divorce, right after I hit the big 4-0, I had to deal with the reality of having to 'trouble' others for the first time. There was no opt-out. I needed help.

Months back, I had felt a lump in my breast, but I was avoiding the truth (much like I avoided my feelings all my life). When I finally got the mammogram, I had not one but three tumors. As this news collided with my contentious divorce and custody battles, I reached my Asian (very tippy) tipping point. I finally admitted that I am NOT fine.

I thought that was the beginning of the end. I had broken nearly every unspoken Chinese taboo. I admitted fault. I admitted I felt ashamed for failing to become a doctor. I admitted I was sick. I admitted I needed help. I admitted I was very unhappy. I admitted I was living someone else's dream for my life. I admitted I didn't even know who I was. I admitted I was full of anger and resentment. I admitted I spent my entire childhood on school and schoolwork at the expense of family relationships, and now I was doing the same by prioritizing my career. I admitted I didn't know what I wanted in life ... but I knew it was NOT being a doctor. I admitted I was scared I'd regret how I spent my time on earth. I was broken.

And then something amazing happened. In the space created through the release of admitting everything that I had felt for years, I felt a tingling of something new. Could it really be ... hope? Even mixed with some excitement? Sprinkled with gratitude? My status quo was crumbling, and it wasn't the end of the world. Rather, it felt as though it could be a new beginning.

Becoming an Advocate for Your Career and Life Design

As I was finishing up my last chemo treatments, I bought myself a pet rabbit (something I'd always wanted as a child but my very clean rodent-phobic mother vetoed). I got my nails done at a high-class salon (my mother would have called it excessive). I bought myself a piano and joined a choir (after years of putting everyone else's needs before my own, I knew that music could help heal my soul). I quit my job in which I felt under-respected and taken advantage of (and, in hindsight, allowed me to keep playing small), and I started my own business (what I'd been dreaming about my whole life). I asked for help (and didn't feel ashamed) and spent a small fortune getting all the support and resources I needed (without the slightest twinge of guilt).

Finally giving myself permission to say: "To hell with everyone else's opinions." I started to be my own advocate for who I REALLY am and what I want to create in my life. I started to live my life ... and I LOVED IT! We're talking the kind of love that ended resting bitch face's 40-year-reign. That kind of only-child-girl-becoming-the-leader-in-her-life kind of love—one that I could feel buzzing through me and out of me and that others could feel when around me.

My external transformation was a reflection of my new internal reality. For the first time in my life, I believed that I AM ENOUGH. I am valuable as a human being. I belong, and I matter. I was done looking for approval from external sources. I had done that all my life, and the only result was it cementing my resting bitch face more and more each day ... and may very well have been the catalyst to my having Stage 2 breast cancer.

My Chinese heritage taught me to be hard-working, respectful, and extremely resilient in adversity. I love that about myself. However, having what I term Internal Integrity™ means that I choose to add to them the pursuit of happiness, empathy for myself and others, as well as valuing family and relationships more than achievement.

Magic happens when we choose to shift "From External Expectations to Internal Integrity." I know you're reading this, asking, "Can I have that transformation too but without cancer?"

In any way that you've been taught excessive humility, self-effacement, deference, or to keep harmony and the status quo at all costs, I want to help you create the internal transformation that empowers you to live your leadership potential.

Creating a new norm begins with thinking differently. Here are 5 examples of how you can reframe cultural training and set the foundation for creating the life YOU desire:

1. ~~"Do what others expect of you, even if it means personal unhappiness."~~ BECOMES "Do what is best for you because your happiness will fuel others' happiness."

2. ~~"Fate deals all of us a bad hand, and our job is to suffer silently. Accept the status quo."~~ BECOMES "The one power stronger than fate is choice, and you always have a choice to change the status quo."

3. ~~"Don't be a nuisance to anyone. To ask for help is to risk being a burden. It's better to be invisible."~~ BECOMES "We all need help. Asking for help doesn't make you a burden; it makes you human."

4. ~~"Your worth as a person is only measured by your grades and which colleges accept you."~~ BECOMES "Your worth is defined on your terms—the limit to which extends as far as you want it to go."

5. ~~"Emotional connection and fulfillment aren't reasonable goals. Bringing your family honor is."~~ BECOMES "Honor begins with letting your heart speak through all of your connections and actions. It's about being true to yourself, along with all those you love."

Don't Settle for Someone Else's Dream!

Look in the mirror deeply and find out who it is that is looking back at you. When you finally become your own advocate and design your career and life as you want it, here's what you'll discover: happiness—the kind that glows through your face each and every day. Goodbye, bitch face; hello, blissful me.

The greatest lesson for me was that I realized when I live with Internal Integrity and embrace who I really am (all of the unclaimed potential that I carried around for so long!), I serendipitously found the alignment of joy, purpose, and peace that I'd wanted all my life. In the end, none of it came through the achievement and approval-seeking culturally ingrained within me ... it came when I set myself free to be me.

ABOUT JEANNY CHAI

BambooMyth.com founder, coach, & speaker, Jeanny Chai, helps Asian American women find their worth from within and "Live Their Leadership Potential" by reframing the cultural priorities that have been given to us. She believes that breaking through the 'bamboo ceiling' is an internal quest, and only by thinking differently can we create a new norm.

Drawing from powerful personal experiences that include 'shaming' her family by not attending medical school after graduating from Stanford, raising four children and becoming known as a successful business development professional in Silicon Valley, Jeanny has devoted herself to helping Asian Americans find their confidence from within. Get ready to transform External Expectations into Internal Integrity™.

It took Jeanny three breast cancer tumors and a divorce to come into the realization of how she could flourish, and she is dedicated to saving other women the pain of having to go through great adversity to reach the point of personal transformation. Read more about Jeanny and her impact at www.bamboomyth.com.

Closing

As you finish the final chapter, we hope you feel what we do—that we aren't done yet!

It has been such an honor to share the stories, the inspirations, the wisdom from these amazing women from around the world. All of these humble women were chosen to share with us because they affected someone's life out there—I know they touched mine. Most of them still don't even realize the impact they may have had and are going to have on other women out there. That's another touch of what makes each of them so special. Just by being themselves, by going out and just DOING what seems RIGHT to do, they are changing the world around them. A world that I know we feel don't always understand us or judges us or is constantly fighting against us. Yet, with all the adversities out there, they don't give up!

It opens your eyes to see that women of all origins, religions, interests, and ages have these things in common—tragedy, triumph, a desire to inspire, a deep yearning to help other women shine. Beautiful things happen when women stop competing and start supporting. Something so strong that we learn to take back our power and not give it up again! It gives real meaning to #metoo. That yes, other women have been in the same situation as you and have made it out—better than before!

Bonding with these women over the last year and a half while we collaborated opened a new window for all of us. Hell, it blew that window out, made room for a new walk-in closet, and cleared the backyard for a she-shed! We hope you are reminded that all the clichés—that you can have it all, that you deserve it, that you are worth it—aren't just clichés. It's work, it's determination, it's not giving up, but it's REAL! So real that I heard every woman's voice as I read their story. I felt their fears, cried their tears, and shouted their cheers. I encourage you to reach out to the women in this book who touched your heart; it's time we all learn to open our mouths and minds positively. Let these women know that their message, their story, is being heard and matters … just like yours does!

Our wish for you is that you rediscover your self-worth and live the life you deserve. All in a good pair of heels.

Love Life ~ Jenny

Power Up, Super Women

Made in the USA
Columbia, SC
19 April 2019